WHSmith

Revise

Maths and English

KS2: YEAR 6

Age 10–11

**Paul Broadbent,
Peter Patilla and
Louis Fidge**

First published 2007
exclusively for WHSmith by
Hodder Murray, a member of the Hodder Headline group
338 Euston Road
London
NW1 3BH

Impression number   10 9 8 7 6 5 4 3 2 1
Year   2008 2007
Text and illustrations © Hodder Education 2007

A CIP record for this book is available from the British Library.

Cover illustration by Sally Newton Illustrations

Typeset by Fakenham Photosetting Limited, Fakenham, Norfolk

ISBN – 13   978 0 34094280 2

Printed and bound in Italy.

Contents

English

The *WHS Revise* series

The *WHS Revise* books enable you to help your child revise and practise important skills taught in school. These skills form part of the National Curriculum and will help your child to improve his or her Maths and English.

Testing in schools

During their time at school all children will undergo a variety of tests. Regular testing is a feature of all schools. It is carried out:

- *informally* – in everyday classroom activities your child's teacher is continually assessing and observing your child's performance in a general way
- *formally* – more regular formal testing helps the teacher check your child's progress in specific areas.

Testing is important because:

- it provides evidence of your child's achievement and progress
- it helps the teacher decide which skills to focus on with your child
- it helps compare how different children are progressing.

The importance of revision

Regular revision is important to ensure your child remembers and practises skills he or she has been taught. These books will help your child revise and test his or her knowledge of some of the things he or she will be expected to know. They will help you prepare your child to be in a better position to face tests in school with confidence.

How to use this book
Units

Each book is divided into a Maths section and an English section. Within each section there are twenty units, each focusing on one key skill. Each unit begins with a **Remember** section, which introduces and revises essential information about the particular skill covered. If possible, read and discuss this with your child to ensure he or she understands it.

This is followed by a **Have a go** section, which contains a number of activities to help your child revise the topic thoroughly and use the skill effectively. Usually, your child should be able to do these activities fairly independently.

Revision tests

There are two revision tests at the end of the Maths section and two revision tests at the end of the English section. These test the skills covered in the preceding units and assess your child's progress and understanding. They can be marked by you or by your child. Your child should fill in his or her test score for each test in the space provided. This will provide a visual record of your child's progress and an instant sense of confidence and achievement.

Parents' notes

The parents' notes (on pages 30–31 for the Maths section and pages 60–61 for the English section) provide you with brief information on each skill and explain why it is important.

Answers

Answers to the unit questions and tests may be found on pages 32–34 (Maths) and pages 62–64 (English).

Unit 1: Rounding decimals

Remember

Rounding to the nearest whole number
- Look at the **tenths** digit.
- If it is 5 or more, round the number up to the next whole number.
- If it is less than 5, the units digit stays the same.

3.5 rounds up to 4
2.49 rounds down to 2

Rounding to the nearest tenth
- Look at the **hundredths** digit.
- If it is 5 or more, round the number up to the next tenth.
- If it is less than 5, the tenths digit stays the same.

1.46 rounds up to 1.5
3.149 rounds down to 3.1

Have a go

1 Round these to the nearest whole number.

a 32.6 ➡ _____   b 17.3 ➡ _____   c 62.9 ➡ _____   d 46.5 ➡ _____

e 27.41 ➡ _____   f 72.63 ➡ _____   g 59.52 ➡ _____   h 6.05 ➡ _____

2 Round these to the nearest tenth.

a 9.33 ➡ _____   b 7.85 ➡ _____   c 2.64 ➡ _____   d 9.16 ➡ _____

e 5.318 ➡ _____   f 2.671 ➡ _____   g 0.809 ➡ _____   h 1.348 ➡ _____

3 Round these weights to the nearest kilogram to work out each approximate total.

a 18.7 kg + 7.44 kg ➡ _____   b 27.09 kg + 35.6 kg ➡ _____

c 56.3 kg + 29.75 kg ➡ _____   d 26.61 kg + 33.05 kg ➡ _____

e 43.46 kg + 25.92 kg ➡ _____   f 19.17 kg + 38.41 kg ➡ _____

4 Estimate which decimal number each arrow points to.

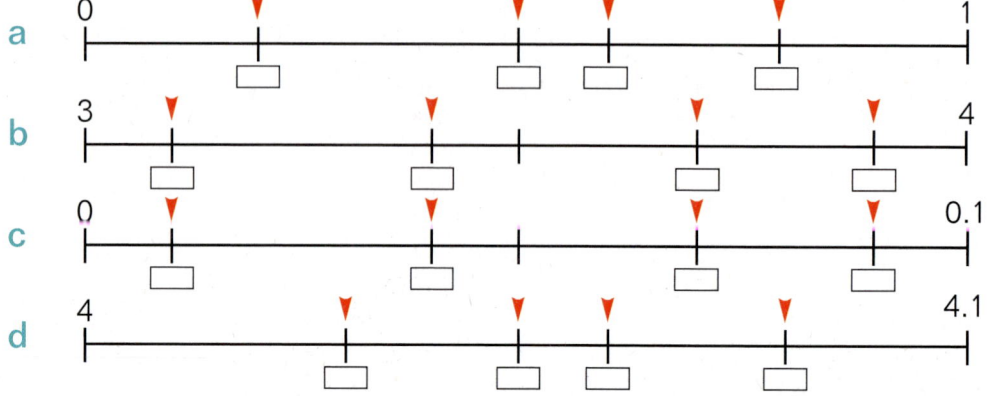

Remember

Function machines can create patterns of results.

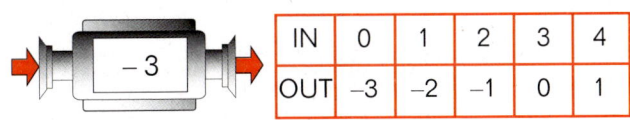

IN	0	1	2	3	4
OUT	−3	−2	−1	0	1

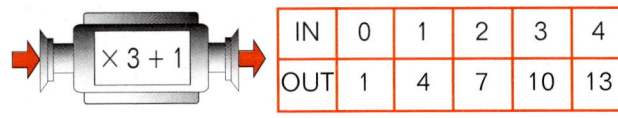

IN	0	1	2	3	4
OUT	1	4	7	10	13

Have a go

1 Complete each table of results.

a

IN	0	1	2	3	4	5	6
OUT							

b

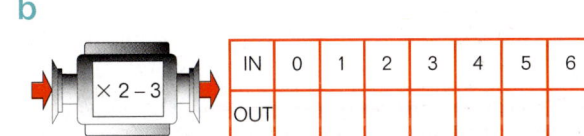

IN	0	1	2	3	4	5	6
OUT							

c

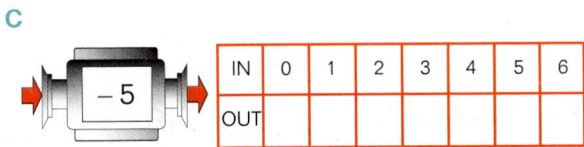

IN	0	1	2	3	4	5	6
OUT							

d

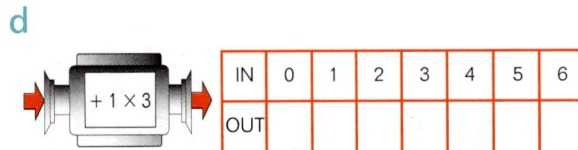

IN	0	1	2	3	4	5	6
OUT							

e

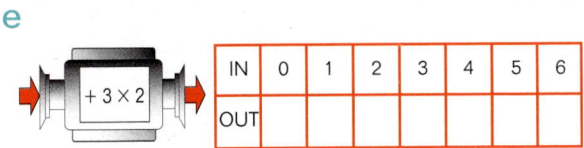

IN	0	1	2	3	4	5	6
OUT							

f

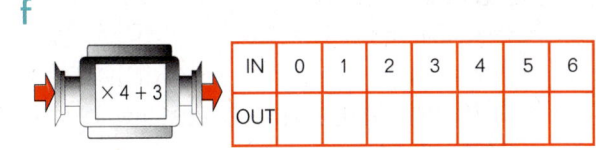

IN	0	1	2	3	4	5	6
OUT							

2 Write the rules for each of these tables of results.

a Rule: _____

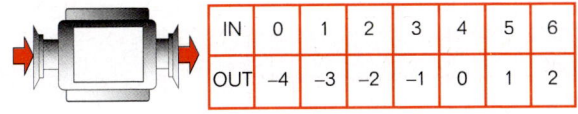

IN	0	1	2	3	4	5	6
OUT	−4	−3	−2	−1	0	1	2

b Rule: _____

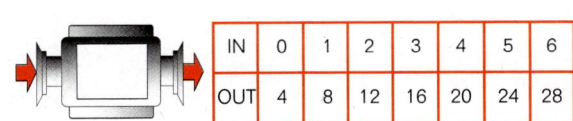

IN	0	1	2	3	4	5	6
OUT	4	8	12	16	20	24	28

c Rule: _____

IN	0	1	2	3	4	5	6
OUT	−2	1	4	7	10	13	16

d Rule: _____

IN	0	1	2	3	4	5	6
OUT	−5	−3	−1	1	3	5	7

Unit 3: Rules of divisibility

Remember

Learn and use these rules of divisibility. A whole number is a multiple of:

2 – if the last digit is even
Examples
26, 214, 3056

3 – if the sum of its digits can be divided by 3
Examples
195 (1 + 9 + 5 = 15),
3045 (3 + 0 + 4 + 5 = 12)

4 – if the last two digits can be divided by 4
Examples
624, 1540, 3764

5 – if the last digit is 0 or 5
Examples
1940, 1335, 6985

6 – if it is even and divisible by 3
Examples
378, 912, 456

8 – if half of it is divisible by 4
Examples
464, 352, 688, 832

9 – if the sum of its digits is divisible by 9
Examples
675, 927, 513, 873

10 – if the last digit is 0
Examples
690, 3050, 9200, 7110

Have a go

1 Look at these dates.

1968   1720   1066   1665   1845   1490   1988   2000

   a Which of these is divisible by 6? _____
   b Which of these is divisible by 8? _____
   c Which dates are divisible by 9? _____
   d Which dates are divisible by 10? _____

2 a Write the dates above in the correct place on this Carroll diagram.

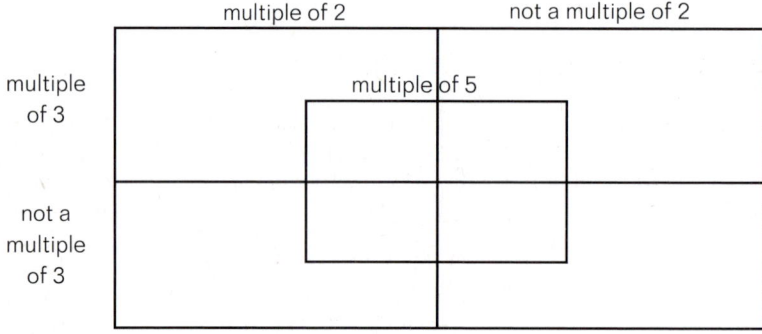

	multiple of 2	not a multiple of 2
multiple of 3	multiple of 5	
not a multiple of 3		

   b Add a year from the 20th century to the Carroll diagram that is divisible by 2, 3 and 5.

Unit 4: Fractions

Remember

Fractions have a numerator and a denominator.

What is $\frac{1}{4}$ of 20?
When the numerator is 1, you divide the number by the denominator.
$\frac{1}{4}$ of 20 = 20 ÷ 4 = 5

What is $\frac{3}{4}$ of 20?
When the numerator is more than 1, you divide by the denominator then multiply by the numerator.
$\frac{1}{4}$ of 20 = 5

$\frac{3}{4}$ of 20 = 5 × 3 = 15

Have a go

1 Answer each of these.

a $\frac{1}{2}$ of…

16 ➡ _____
28 ➡ _____
40 ➡ _____
52 ➡ _____

b $\frac{1}{4}$ of…

24 ➡ _____
60 ➡ _____
4 ➡ _____
100 ➡ _____

c $\frac{1}{5}$ of…

30 ➡ _____
15 ➡ _____
70 ➡ _____
120 ➡ _____

d $\frac{1}{8}$ of…

16 ➡ _____
56 ➡ _____
80 ➡ _____
160 ➡ _____

e $\frac{2}{3}$ of…

15 ➡ _____
27 ➡ _____
60 ➡ _____
45 ➡ _____
99 ➡ _____

f $\frac{4}{5}$ of…

40 ➡ _____
25 ➡ _____
65 ➡ _____
110 ➡ _____
150 ➡ _____

g $\frac{3}{4}$ of…

28 ➡ _____
80 ➡ _____
32 ➡ _____
96 ➡ _____
44 ➡ _____

h $\frac{3}{10}$ of…

120 ➡ _____
500 ➡ _____
90 ➡ _____
200 ➡ _____
150 ➡ _____

2 Circle the greater amount in each pair.

a
$\frac{1}{2}$ of £6 or
$\frac{1}{4}$ of £20

b
$\frac{3}{10}$ of £7 or
$\frac{2}{3}$ of £3

c
$\frac{3}{5}$ of £8 or
$\frac{3}{4}$ of £6

d
$\frac{2}{5}$ of £2.20
or $\frac{3}{4}$ of £1.60

e
$\frac{2}{3}$ of £2.10
or $\frac{1}{5}$ of £7.20

f
$\frac{4}{5}$ of £10 or
$\frac{7}{10}$ of £12

Unit 5: Percentages

Remember

If you know how to work out percentages of amounts, then you can work out discounts and sale prices.

A pair of shoes which normally costs £28 is in a sale with 20% off. What is the sale price?

Step 1
Work out the percentage:
20% of £28:
10% is £2.80, so
20% of £28 is £5.60

Step 2
Take away this amount from the price:
£28.00 – £5.60 is £22.40

So the sale price is £22.40.

Have a go

1 Calculate the sale price of each of these.

a

10% REDUCTION

£14

£36

Sale price:
£ _____

Sale price:
£ _____

£68

£8.20

Sale price:
£ _____

Sale price:
£ _____

b
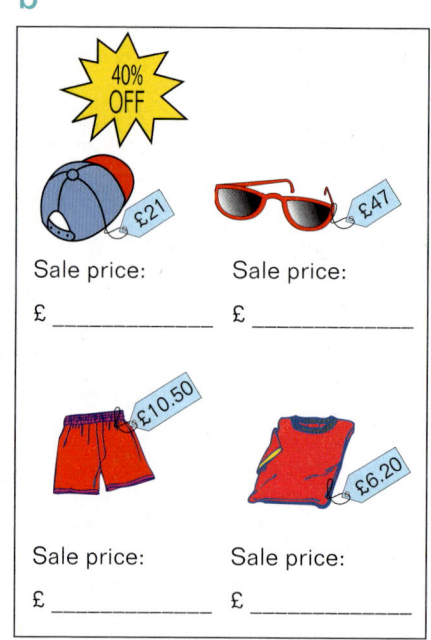

40% OFF

£21

£47

Sale price:
£ _____

Sale price:
£ _____

£10.50

£6.20

Sale price:
£ _____

Sale price:
£ _____

c
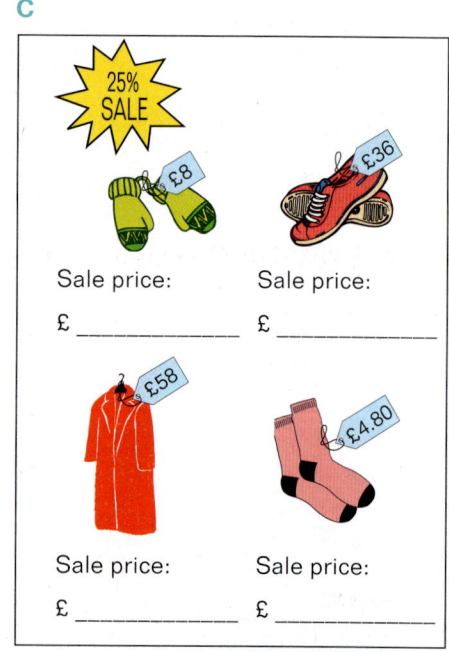

25% SALE

£8

£36

Sale price:
£ _____

Sale price:
£ _____

£58

£4.80

Sale price:
£ _____

Sale price:
£ _____

2 A travel company has two special offers on a holiday for a week in Greece, which normally costs £714 for a family of four.

Which saves more money? _____

I would choose Offer _____ because

_____ .

GREECE

Special Deal

CHOOSE ONE OF THESE WAYS TO SAVE MONEY

Offer 1
Pay before March and
15% discount

Offer 2
Pay before March and get
£100 off your holiday

Unit 6: Equations

Remember

Equations use letters or symbols instead of numbers, which need to be worked out.

$x - 5 = 7$
Use addition: $7 + 5 = 12$
So $x = 12$

$2a = 8$
This means 2 times a equals 8.
$2 \times 4 = 8$, so $a = 4$

$3y + 2 = 8$
Take away 2 from 8 and you are left with 6.
Divide 6 by 3 and $y = 2$

Have a go

1 Write in the missing numbers.

a $7 + \boxed{} = 15$

b $19 - \boxed{} = 11$

c $\boxed{} + 6 = 13$

d $3 \times \boxed{} = 15$

e $(2 \times \boxed{}) - 5 = 1$

f $12 - (2 \times \boxed{}) = 2$

g $(4 \times \boxed{}) + 6 = 14$

h $8 + (3 \times \boxed{}) = 20$

2 Write the value of each letter.

a $8 + y = 17$
$y =$ _____

b $n - 4 = 11$
$n =$ _____

c $12 - x = 3$
$x =$ _____

d $6a = 18$
$a =$ _____

e $c + 9 = 20$
$c =$ _____

f $3b - 1 = 11$
$b =$ _____

g $4x + 5 = 25$
$x =$ _____

h $14 - 3z = 8$
$z =$ _____

i $7y - 4 = 17$
$y =$ _____

j $13 + 6a = 43$
$a =$ _____

3 If $a = 5$, $b = 2$, $c = 3$, $x = 6$ and $y = 4$, work out the value of each of these:

a $4a + b =$ _____

b $3x - y =$ _____

c $a + b + c =$ _____

d $2b + 3y =$ _____

e $2y - 3b =$ _____

f $4c + 2a =$ _____

g $(4b - 5) + c =$ _____

h $y + (2x - a) =$ _____

Remember

When we add **decimals** that are too large to total in our heads, we use a written method, like this.

```
  37.48
+ 78.90
------
 116.38
  1 1 1
```

For this method, line up the decimal points and then start at the right-hand column.

Have a go

1 Answer each of these.

a
```
    3.68
+ 29.36
------
```

b
```
   28.93
+ 17.8
------
```

c
```
    4.27
+ 37.96
------
```

d
```
   28.49
+ 51.07
------
```

e
```
   34.93
+ 27.8
------
```

f
```
     4.89
+ 159.72
------
```

g
```
    39.93
+ 125.8
------
```

h
```
   93.85
+ 49.48
------
```

i
```
   208.9
+ 84.66
------
```

j
```
   38.78
+ 52.37
------
```

2 Here are the prices of some DIY items:

£17.25   £43.89   £29.52   £14.65   £128.90

Write the total cost of the items on each of these shopping lists.

a

```
Ladder _____
Wheelbarrow _____

Total: _____
```

b

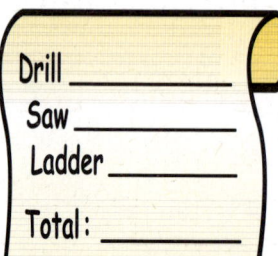

```
Drill _____
Saw _____
Ladder _____

Total: _____
```

c

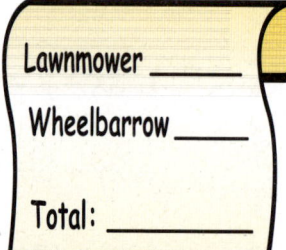

```
Lawnmower _____
Wheelbarrow _____

Total: _____
```

d

```
Drill _____
Wheelbarrow_____
Saw _____

Total: _____
```

Unit 8: Subtraction of decimals

Remember

When we subtract **decimals** that are too large to work out in our heads, we use a written method, like this.

$$
\begin{array}{r}
{\scriptstyle 6^1\ \ 5^1} \\
7\cancel{3}.\cancel{6}3 \\
-\ 38.24 \\
\hline
35.39 \\
\hline
\end{array}
$$

For this subtraction, you need to change tenths to hundredths and tens to units.

Have a go

1 Answer each of these.

a	b	c	d	e
34.90 − 15.62	78.16 − 19.80	50.27 − 17.39	36.19 − 28.07	54.38 − 26.85

f	g	h	i	j
52.03 − 39.78	184.30 − 95.82	106.87 − 58.90	117.45 − 83.69	128.08 − 72.87

2 Here are the prices of some clothes:

£32.65 trousers   £128.39 suit   £18.42 shirt   £46.18 jacket   £27.85 jumper   £9.54 shorts

a What change from £20 would you get if you bought a shirt? £

b What is the difference in price between the shorts and the trousers? £

c How much more expensive is the suit than the jacket? £

d How much cheaper is the shirt than the jumper? £

e Two items are bought and the total cost is £3.73 less than £50. Which two items are they? _____ and _____

Remember

When you multiply by a number that is less than 1, the answer will be less than the value you started with.

$39 \times 0.4 = 15.6$.

Always estimate an approximate answer first.

0.4 is almost $\frac{1}{2}$, and $\frac{1}{2}$ of 40 is 20, so 39×0.4 will be a little less than 20.

Have a go

1 Join each calculation to the correct answer.

0.17 × 0.4	0.068	0.08 × 7
0.8 × 0.7	0.56	1.7 × 0.4
8 × 0.7	5.6	0.17 × 4
0.8 × 7	6.8	17 × 0.4
1.7 × 4	56	80 × 0.7
	0.68	

2 Multiply each of these by any whole number less than 10.
Make each answer as near to 100 as you can – it can be just above or just below 100.

a 31.7 × ☐ = ☐   b 18.5 × ☐ = ☐   c 11.7 × ☐ = ☐

d 12.9 × ☐ = ☐   e 49.1 × ☐ = ☐   f 15.8 × ☐ = ☐

g 24.7 × ☐ = ☐   h 14.4 × ☐ = ☐

Remember

If you need to multiply two numbers together that are too difficult to work out in your head, try using the grid method.

Example: 364 × 52

1 Write them round a grid as hundreds, tens and ones.
2. Multiply each pair of numbers to complete the grid.
3. Add up the rows in the grid.
4. Add up the totals.

	300	60	4
50	15000	3000	200
2	600	120	8

→ 18200
+ 728
18928

It is always a good idea to work out an approximate answer first.

Have a go

1 Use the grid method to answer these.

a 3 2 8
   × 2 4

	300	20	8
20			
4			

b 1 8 9
   × 4 6

	100	80	9
40			
6			

c 4 5 3
   × 5 7

	400	50	3
50			
7			

d 5 1 9
   × 4 8

	500	10	9
40			
8			

2 Use the digits in this calculation.

[4] [7] [9] [6] [3]

☐☐☐ × ☐☐ = ?

Arrange the digits to make:

a The largest possible answer ➡ __ __ __ × __ __ = _____

b The smallest possible answer ➡ __ __ __ × __ __ = _____

Unit 11: Long division

Remember

A quotient is an answer to a division. This is one way to calculate a division with big numbers:

840 ÷ 35

```
        24
  35 | 840
      700   (35 × 20)
      140
      140   (35 × 4)
```

Have a go

1 Answer these.

a   b   c   d

15 | 585   14 | 896   18 | 828   23 | 782

e   f   g   h

17 | 1156   29 | 1653   34 | 1564   36 | 2448

2 Calculate the length of side x for each of these rectangles.

a

32 cm

x | Area = 896 cm²

x = _____

b

27 cm

x | Area = 486 cm²

x = _____

c

x

Area = 676 cm² | 26 cm

x = _____

d

38 cm

x | Area = 874 cm²

x = _____

e

x

Area = 893 cm² | 19 cm

x = _____

f

18 cm

Area = 306 cm² | x

x = _____

g

26 cm

Area = 520 cm² | x

x = _____

h

x

Area = 648 cm² | 18 c

x = _____

Unit 12: Lines and polygons

Remember

Parallel lines will never meet – they are always the same distance apart.

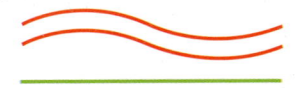

Lines which are parallel are often marked with arrows.

Diagonals are lines that join any two vertices (corners) of a shape.

 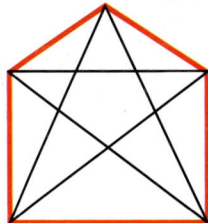

Have a go

Complete this table of polygons.
Sketch each shape and mark any parallel lines, diagonals and right angles.
Tick each part of the table if it is true and put a cross if it is untrue.
The first one has been done for you.

Shape	Sketch	Parallel sides	All sides equal	Three or more diagonals	Right angles
Rectangle		✓	✗	✗	✓
Equilateral triangle					
Rhombus					
Parallelogram					
Regular hexagon					
Trapezium					
Regular pentagon					

Remember

Polyhedrons are 3D solids made from many polygons.

Each polyhedron has:

- a face which is flat and is a polygon
- an edge which is a straight line where two faces meet
- a vertex which is the point where three or more edges meet.

Have a go

1 Join these descriptions to the correct names.

4 rectangle faces and 2 square faces	cuboid	6 square faces
1 square face and 4 triangle faces	square-based pyramid	2 pentagon faces and 5 rectangle faces
	cube	
	triangular prism	
4 triangle faces	tetrahedron	2 triangle faces and 3 rectangle faces
	pentagonal prism	

2 Each polyhedron has a number of faces, edges and vertices. Complete this chart for each shape.

Shape		Number of faces	Number of edges	Number of vertices
Cube		6	12	8
Cuboid				
Tetrahedron				
Square-based pyramid				
Pentagonal prism				
Triangular prism				

Can you spot a rule or pattern linking the number of faces, edges and vertices?

Unit 14: Symmetry

Remember

Shapes are symmetrical if both sides match when a mirror line or a line of symmetry is drawn.

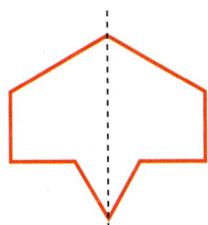

Have a go

Add one extra triangle to each shape. The finished shape must have a line of symmetry.

Draw the lines of symmetry on each shape.

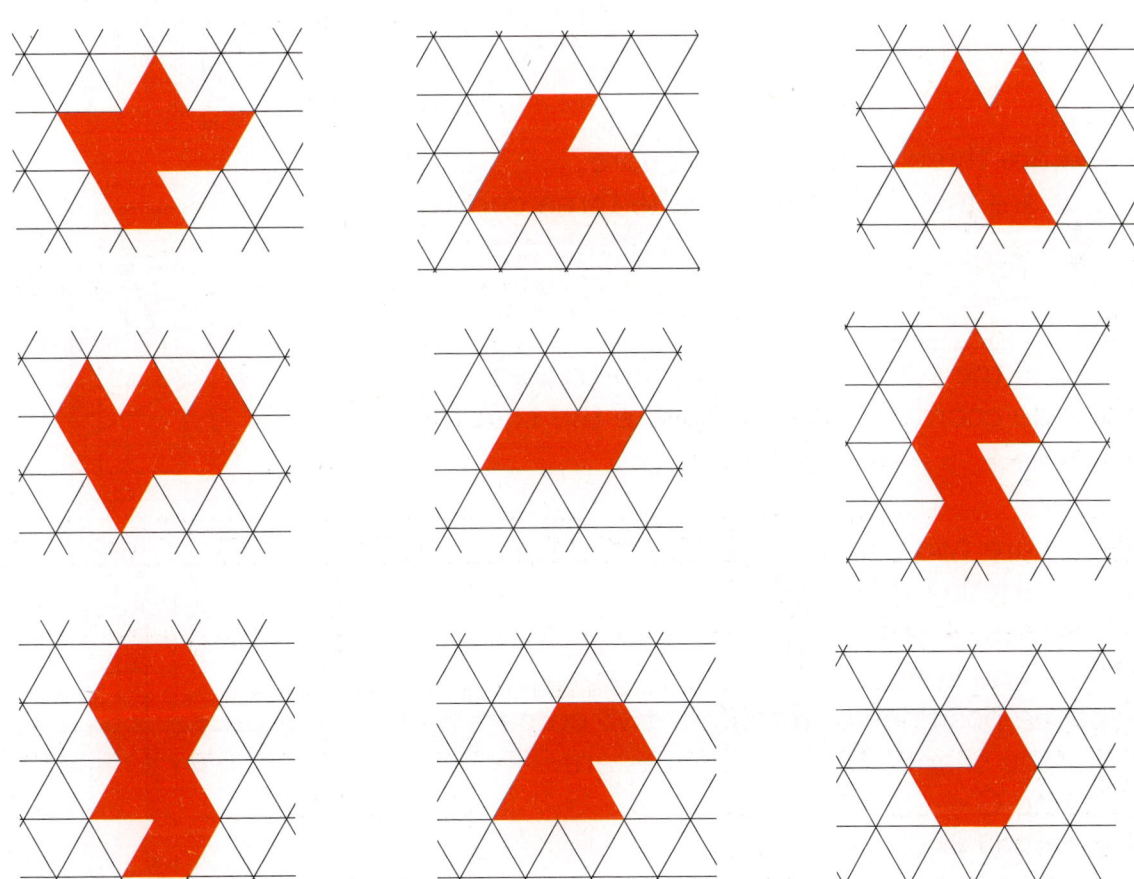

Colour each shape with different colours.
Make a symmetrical pattern for each of them.

Unit 15: Coordinates

Remember

A **coordinate** shows an exact position
of a point on a grid. Negative numbers
can be used to show positions.
The coordinates of A are (−2, −1)
The coordinates of B are (3, −4)
The coordinates of C are (−1, −3)
Read the horizontal coordinate first and then the vertical coordinate.

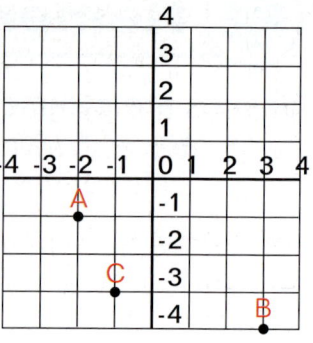

Have a go

1 Plot the points below and join them in order.
Name the shape.
(−2, 4) (3, 0) (0, −4) (−5, 0)

Shape : _____

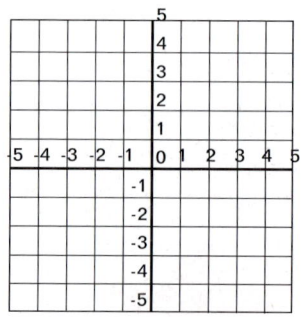

2 Here are three corners of a square.
What are the coordinates of the three corners?
A ➡ (___,___)
B ➡ (___,___)
C ➡ (___,___)
What is the coordinate of the fourth corner, D? (___,___)
Plot the coordinate and complete the square.

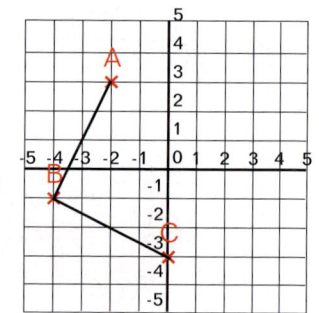

3 These are two corners of a quadrilateral.
What are the coordinates for:
a Position A ➡ (___,___)
b Position B ➡ (___,___)
Plot the positions of the other two corners and
draw the shape. The coordinates are:
Position C ➡ (5, −4)
Position D ➡ (0, −4)

Name the shape : _____

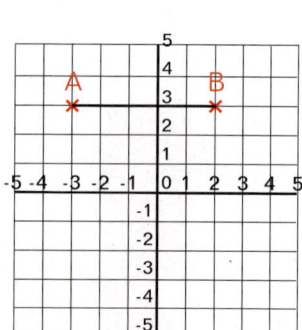

Unit 16: Measures

Remember

We still sometimes use imperial measures.
These include pints, gallons, pounds, inches and feet.

Length	Weight	Capacity
12 inches = 1 foot	16 ounces = 1 pound (lb)	8 pints = 1 gallon
2.5 cm ≈ 1 inch	25 g ≈ 1 ounce	1 litre ≈ 1.75 pints
30 cm ≈ 1 foot	1 kg ≈ 2.25 lb	4.5 litres ≈ 1 gallon
1 metre ≈ 3.25 feet	1 lb ≈ 450 g	1 pint ≈ 550 ml
1.6 km ≈ 1 mile		

Remember that ≈ means 'is approximately equal to.'

Have a go

1 Change these to approximate metric units.

a

4 gallons

b

Bolton 20 miles

c

9 lb

d

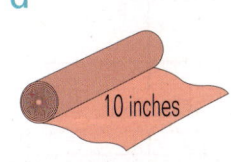
10 inches

e

3 PINTS

f

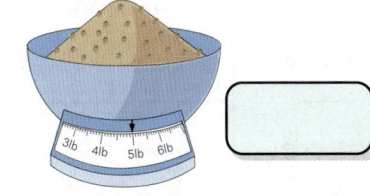

2 Here is a conversion graph for litres to pints.
1 litre = 1.75 pints

Use the graph to complete this table. Conversions are approximate.

Litres	1		6		2	
Pints		5		8		4

Unit 17: Timetables

Remember

Read timetables carefully.
They are often on a grid,
so make sure that you read across
the rows and down the columns for
the correct times.

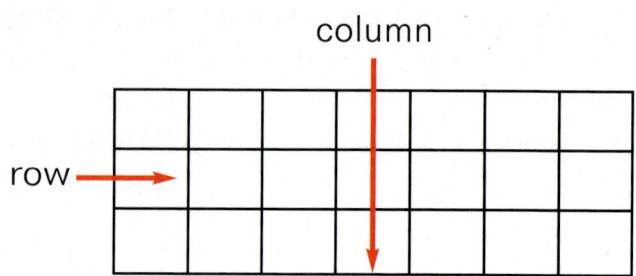

column

row

Have a go

This is Jamie's secondary school timetable for the week.

		8:50 9:00	9:50	10:40	11:00	11:50	12:40	1:40 1:50	2:40	3:30
		Lesson 1	Lesson 2		Lesson 3	Lesson 4			Lesson 5	Lesson 6
Mon	R E G I S T R A T I O N	Geography	French	B R E A K	Maths	P.E.	L U N C H	R E G I S T R A T I O N	English	Science
Tue		Design/Technology			History	Maths			R.E.	French
Wed		English	History		Maths	Geography			Games	
Thurs		Science			English	Maths			Art	
Fri		Maths	P.S.E.		German	English			French	Science

Use this timetable to answer these questions.

a How many minutes is each single lesson? _____

b How long is the lunch break? _____

c What is Jamie's first lesson after break on a Friday? _____

d What does Jamie do for Lesson 5 on a Monday? _____

e How many minutes are spent on English each week? _____

f How much time is spent out of lessons each day? _____

g How many more minutes does Jamie spend in maths than science?

_____

h How many minutes are there between break and lunch? _____

Unit 18: Area of triangles

Remember

Area of a rectangle = length × width
$A = l \times w$

4 cm

3 cm

Area = 4 cm × 3 cm = 12 cm²

To find the area of a **right-angled triangle**, make it into a rectangle and then halve the area of the rectangle.

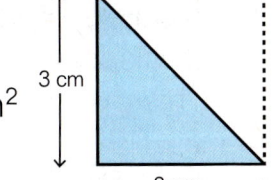

3 cm

3 cm

Area = 3 cm × 3 cm = 9 cm²
$\frac{1}{2}$ of 9 = 4.5 cm²
Area of triangle is 4.5 cm²

Have a go

1 Calculate the shaded areas.

a
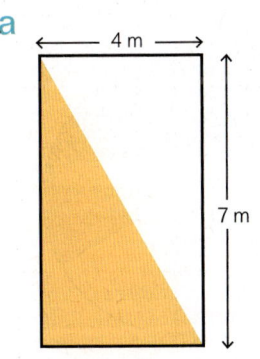
4 m

7 m

Area = _____

b
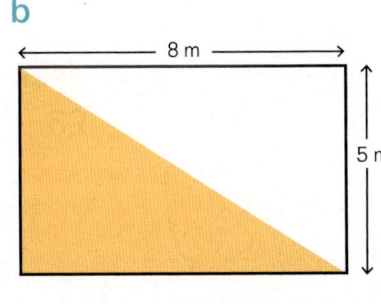
8 m

5 m

Area = _____

c
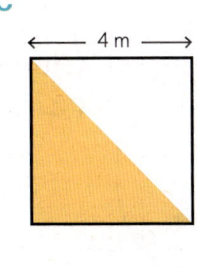
4 m

Area = _____

d
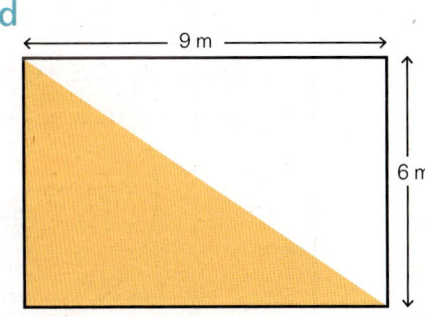
9 m

6 m

Area = _____

2 Calculate the area of these triangles.

a
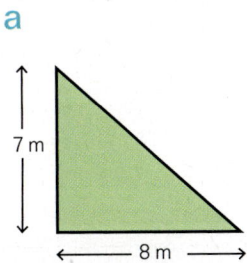
7 m

8 m

Area = _____

b
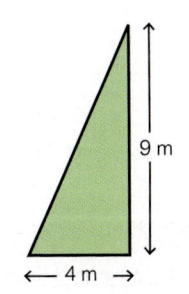
9 m

4 m

Area = _____

c
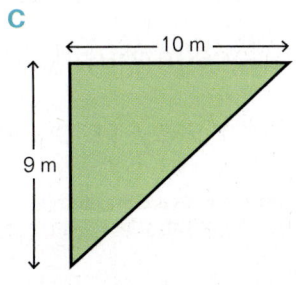
10 m

9 m

Area = _____

d
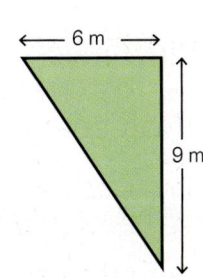
6 m

9 m

Area = _____

Unit 19: Pie charts

Remember

Pie charts are circles divided into sections. Each section shows a number of items. Always look at the total for the whole 'pie' and then work out the fraction of each section.

A survey of 30 children was carried out to discover their favourite types of crisps. This pie chart shows the results.
$\frac{1}{5}$ of the children chose smoky bacon as their favourite flavour. There were 30 children altogether, so $\frac{1}{5}$ of 30 is 6 children. How many chose prawn cocktail?

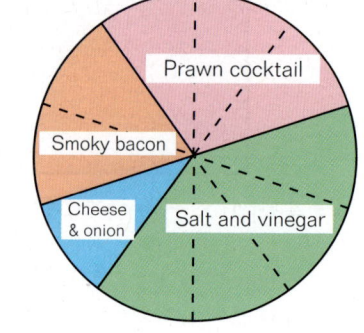

Have a go

These pie charts show how each child used their pocket money in a week.

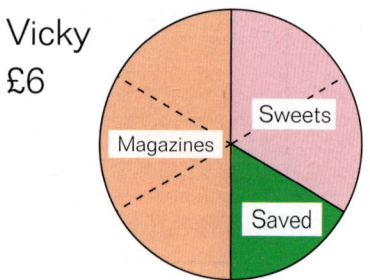
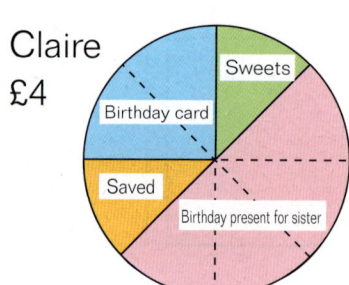
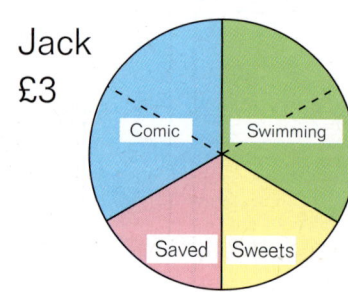

a How much did Jack spend on his comic? _____

b Which two children both saved 50p of their pocket money?

_____ and _____

c How much were Vicky's magazines? _____

d Who spent the most money on sweets? _____

e How much more did Vicky save than Jack? _____

f What fraction of his pocket money did Jack spend on swimming?

_____

g How much did Claire spend on a birthday present for her sister? _____

h What fraction of her pocket money did Claire spend on a

birthday card? _____

Remember

Exchange rates show the value of one currency against another.
The euro is now used by many European countries.

£1 is approximately equal to €1.67.

This graph shows the conversion between the euro and pounds sterling.

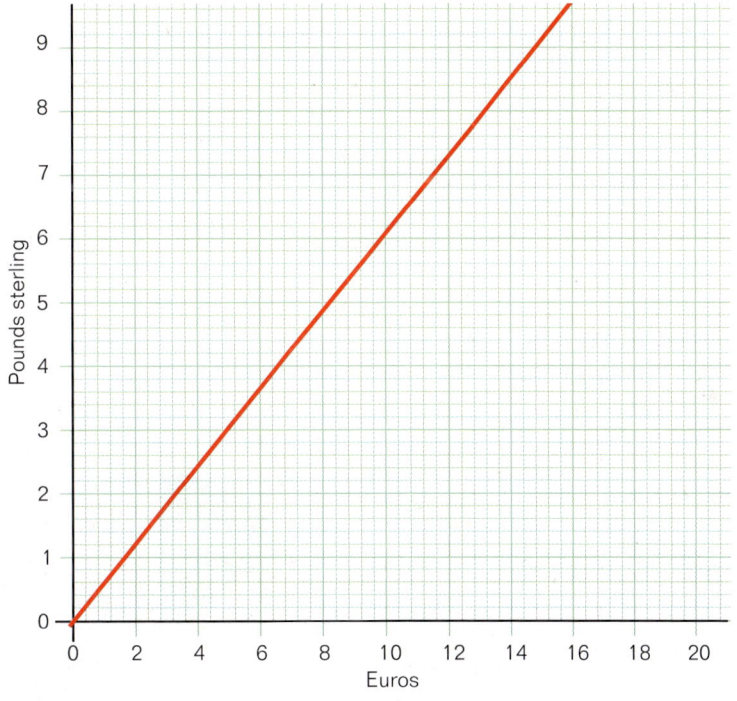

1 Use the graph to convert these euros to pounds:

a €4.00 = £ ____   b €9.00 = £ ____   c €5.00 = £ ____   d €6.00 = £ ____
e €2.50 = £ ____   f €0.50 = £ ____   g €7.50 = £ ____   h €9.50 = £ ____

2 Use the graph to convert these pounds to euros:

a £1.20 = € ____   b £4.80 = € ____   c £4.20 = € ____   d £6.00 = € ____
e £0.90 = € ____   f £2.10 = € ____   g £5.10 = € ____   h £3.90 = € ____

3 Look in a newspaper to find the current exchange rate for euros and pounds sterling. Draw a second conversion line (in a different colour) on this graph to show the rate.

Test 1

Check how much you have learned.

Answer the questions.
Mark your answers. Fill in your score.

SCORE

1 Round these numbers:
   a 8.35
   – to the nearest whole number ➡ _____
   – to the nearest tenth ➡ _____

   b 42.64
   – to the nearest whole number ➡ _____
   – to the nearest tenth ➡ _____

out of 4

2 Write the rule and complete the table of results.

IN	0	1	2	3	4	5	6
OUT	–3	1	5	9	__	__	__

Rule: _____

out of 2

3 Convert these amounts.
   a 6 feet ≈ _____ metres
   b 4 ounces ≈ _____ grams
   c 2 gallons ≈ _____ litres

out of 3

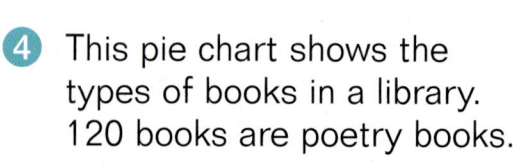

4 This pie chart shows the
types of books in a library.
120 books are poetry books.

Poetry

Fiction

Non-fiction

   a How many books are fiction? _____
   b What fraction of the books are non-fiction? _____

out of 2

5 Write the value of n.
   a $n - 4 = 11$ b $4n - 5 = 19$
   $n =$ _____ $n =$ _____

out of 2

6 What is $\frac{3}{5}$ of £4.50? _____

out of 1

7 Show the pairs of parallel lines on each of these shapes.

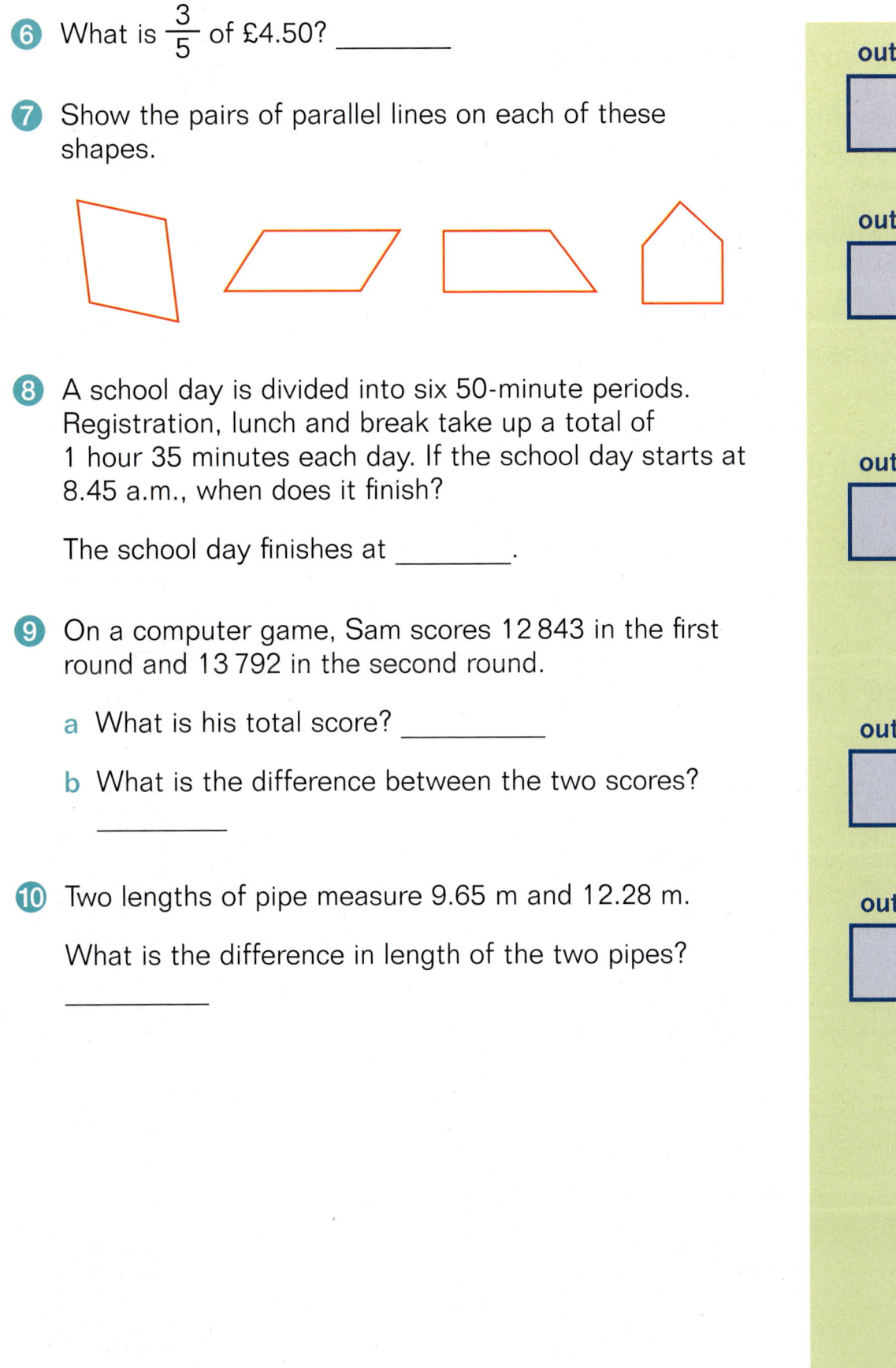

out of 2

8 A school day is divided into six 50-minute periods. Registration, lunch and break take up a total of 1 hour 35 minutes each day. If the school day starts at 8.45 a.m., when does it finish?

The school day finishes at _____.

out of 1

9 On a computer game, Sam scores 12 843 in the first round and 13 792 in the second round.

a What is his total score? _____

b What is the difference between the two scores?

_____

out of 2

10 Two lengths of pipe measure 9.65 m and 12.28 m.

What is the difference in length of the two pipes?

_____

out of 1

Total out of 20

Test 2

Check how much you have learned.

Answer the questions.
Mark your answers. Fill in your score.

1 Look at these numbers.

3160   2463   1845   3400   2615

Circle the number which is a common multiple of both 3 and 5.

out of 1

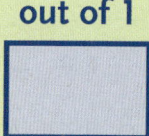

2 Calculate the area of this triangle.

_____

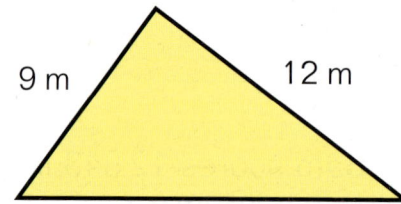

9 m   12 m

out of 1

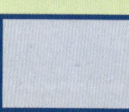

3 Answer this.

4 5 9
× 4 3

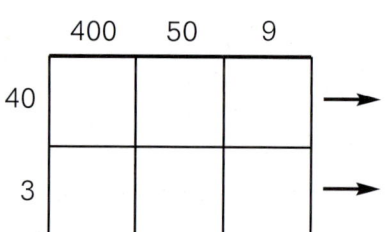

400   50   9

40

3

out of 2

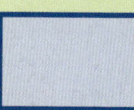

4 Answer these.

out of 2

a
18)612

b
26)1924

5 Complete the sentence for this shape.

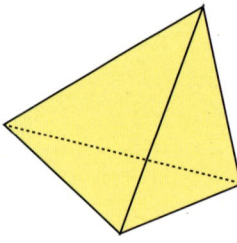

A _____ has _____ faces,

_____ edges and _____ vertices.

out of 2

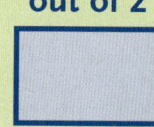

6 Write the answers.

    a 12 × 0.9 = _____   b 0.8 × 0.6 = _____

    c 6.4 × 0.3 = _____

7 A tennis racket costs £56. In a sale this is reduced by 30%.

    What is the sale price of the tennis racket? _____

8 Draw the lines of symmetry on this shape.

9 This graph shows the conversion between the US dollar and pounds sterling.
£1 is approximately equal to $1.40.
Use the graph to answer these.

    a £4.50 ➡ $ _____   b $9.80 ➡ £ _____

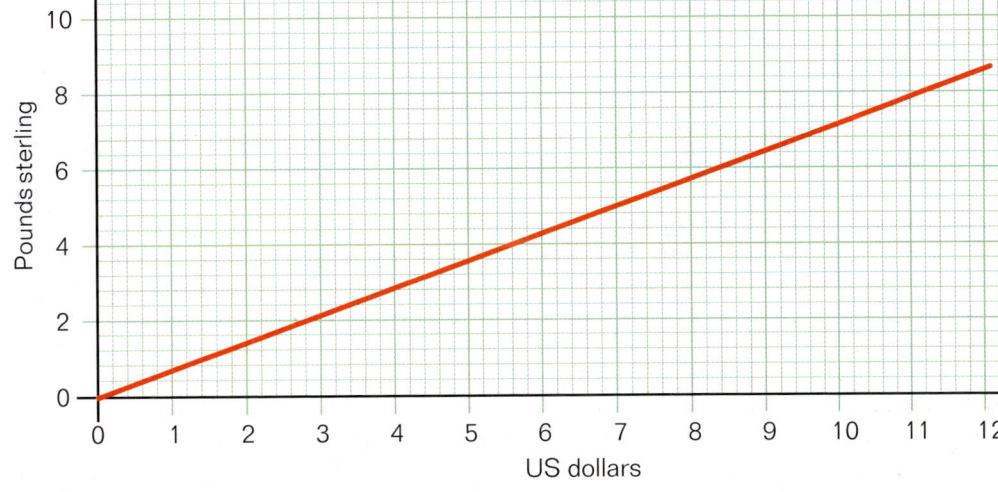

Parents' notes (Maths)

Unit 1: Rounding decimals   Being able to round decimal numbers to the nearest whole number or tenth is a useful skill, particularly when trying to work out approximate answers to tricky calculations. Read through the rules for rounding, making sure that your child knows the difference between rounding to the nearest whole number and rounding to the nearest tenth.

Unit 2: Functions and patterns   A function is a rule for changing one set of numbers into another set. A function machine can show functions by having numbers going into the machine, following the rule or function, and coming out of the machine. Single operations, such as $\times 4$ or $+5$ are fairly easy to see from the numbers, but two-stage operations such as $\times 2 + 3$ are more difficult. Remind your child to carry out the operations in order to work out the numbers coming out. To work out the function from numbers going into and coming out of a machine, look at the relationship between each pair of numbers and try to work out the rule for changing each of them.

Unit 3: Rules of divisibility   Your child should recognise multiples of different numbers to 10. Make sure that he or she understands that multiples don't stop at $10 \times$ a number, but go on and on. The important thing is to recognise the 'rule' for a set of multiples. These are called 'rules of divisibility', used to recognise whether a large number can be divided by, or is a multiple of, a certain number. For example, we know that 1384 is a multiple of 4 because the last two digits are a multiple of 4. Note there is no rule for multiples of 7.

Unit 4: Fractions   Check that your child knows that the number above the line of a fraction is the numerator and the number below the line is the denominator. When the numerator is 1, to find a fraction of an amount you simply divide by the denominator. So $\frac{1}{5}$ of 30 is the same as $30 \div 5$, which is 6. If the numerator is more than 1, you multiply by the numerator as well. So $\frac{4}{5}$ of 30 is the same as 30 $\div 5$ (which is 6), then multiplied by 4, which is 24.

Unit 5: Percentages   Percentages are simply fractions out of 100. To calculate discounts and sale prices, you need to work out percentages of amounts. A good method is to use 10% to help work it out. Go through the example to follow the method. Make sure that your child knows that once he or she has worked out the percentage, this gives the amount to be discounted. Your child must then subtract this from the original cost to work out the sale price.

Unit 6: Equations   Equations use letters or symbols instead of numbers in a calculation. They are often less complicated than they appear and, if your child has worked on a lot of missing-number problems, they can usually be solved quickly. If the letters cause confusion, ask your child to draw a square around the letter so that it looks like an empty box. Your child can then put a number into the box and read the whole equation to see if it is correct. If it is the wrong number, he or she can then try another in the same way.

Unit 7: Addition of decimals   When adding two numbers, always encourage your child to look at the numbers first to see if they can be added mentally. If the numbers are too complicated, then your child will need to use a written method. There are several different written methods, and this 'vertical' method is just one particular example. It may be that your child wants to make informal jottings of numbers as they are added or he or she may prefer the formal method shown. Go through each step carefully, making sure that the columns and decimal points are lined up.

Unit 8: Subtraction of decimals   As with addition, always encourage your child to look at the numbers first to see if they can be subtracted mentally. If your child needs to use a written method he or she can choose between the formal method shown, or use another method. The 'vertical' method is called decomposition, where numbers are 'exchanged' to make them easier to work with. An alternative is to find the difference between two numbers, counting on from the smaller number to the next ten and then on to the larger number.

Unit 9 Multiplying decimals   When multiplying by decimals less than 1, it is important for your child to understand that the answer will be smaller than the number you started with. To check this, multiply 16 by 0.5, relating this to $\frac{1}{2}$ of 16. Before calculating each answer, make sure that your child estimates an approximate answer. Your child needs to be confident at multiplying, and also have a good understanding of place value.

Unit 10: Multiplication – grid method   Multiplying by large numbers is more difficult to do mentally, but the grid method works well on paper. It involves breaking numbers up and multiplying each part. Go through each of the four stages carefully, making sure that your child understands the method. Practise it so that it becomes a quick and accurate method, and a good alternative to the written vertical method.

Unit 11: Long division   Written division methods are quite tricky, so it is important that your child is confident at dividing numbers mentally, knows the multiplication tables, and can multiply larger numbers quickly. This will help speed up the stages in working out a written division and allow your child to concentrate on the process. Encourage your child to estimate an approximate answer first.

Unit 12: Lines and polygons   Polygons are two-dimensional shapes with straight sides. Each has a special name related to the number of sides, so, for example, a shape with six straight sides is a hexagon. Each polygon has certain properties, and this unit focuses on parallel lines and diagonals. Your child has to look for shapes with parallel sides and check the number of diagonals. You could also ask your child to look for shapes with diagonals that cross each other at right angles (for example, the square and rhombus).

Unit 13: 3D solids   Your child will need to be able to recognise and name polyhedra and describe their properties, including knowing the shapes of the faces (polygons). This will also involve counting the number of faces, edges and vertices (corners). There is a relationship between these for each polyhedron. Euler, an eighteenth-century Swiss mathematician, discovered the formula: number of faces + number of vertices – number of edges = 2. So, for a cube: $6 + 8 - 12 = 2$.

Unit 14: Symmetry   The mirror line or line of symmetry is best thought of as a line that cuts a shape into two identical pieces. If a mirror is placed on the line, the whole shape can be seen when you look in the mirror. Some shapes only have one line of symmetry, but other shapes have more, such as equilateral triangles and regular hexagons.

Unit 15: Coordinates   A common error when reading coordinates is to get the two numbers the wrong way round. In the example, position (3, –4) is shown as B. Encourage your child to start at zero and go across the horizontal x-axis until level with B (across 3) and then down to B (down 4). This will get your child into the habit of reading across the x-axis (left or right) before going up or down the y-axis.

Unit 16: Measures   Imperial measures are still sometimes used for measuring length (miles, feet and inches), weight (pounds and ounces) and capacity (gallons and pints). Talk about the times and places where these units are still used and try to give your child an idea of the approximate equivalence of them to metric units of measure.

Unit 17: Timetables   When your child starts secondary school, he or she will be expected to follow a timetable. Try to get an example of one from an older pupil and look at the layout and times. Use the example in this unit to look at the length of each lesson and the times of the breaks and lunch, as well as the start and finish times. Ask your child what could be done to make the timetable quick and easy to use – for example, using different colour coding.

Unit 18: Area of triangles   Your child should be able to use the formula for working out the area of a rectangle. Make sure that your child understands that we use just the initial letters to represent the words – for example, l is length and b is breadth. Once your child knows how to work out the area of a rectangle, the area of a right-angled triangle is easy, as it is half of a rectangle. If your child learns that it is $\frac{1}{2}$ (base $\times$ height) then this will help him or her when working out the area of any right-angled triangle.

Unit 19: Pie charts   Pie charts are a useful type of chart for comparing different values. They are not always easy to read, particularly when you need to work out actual amounts, so encourage your child to read all the information given. This will include a total for the whole 'pie', from which each sector can be calculated. Make sure that your child works out the fraction of the whole amount for each sector.

Unit 20: Conversion graphs   Exchange rates around Europe have been made a lot simpler since the introduction of the euro. This conversion graph plots pounds sterling against the euro. Make sure that your child understands how to read the graph, reading up and across from the line to convert one currency to the other for different values.

Answers (Maths)

Unit 1: Rounding decimals (page 6)

1 a 33   b 17   c 63
   d 47   e 27   f 73
   g 60   h 6

2 a 9.3   b 7.9   c 2.6
   d 9.2   e 5.3   f 2.7
   g 0.8   h 1.3

3 a 26 kg   b 63 kg   c 86 kg
   d 60 kg   e 69 kg   f 57 kg

4 a 0.2   0.5   0.6   0.8
   b 3.1   3.4   3.7   3.9
   c 0.01   0.04   0.07   0.09
   d 4.03   4.05   4.06   4.08

Unit 2: Functions and patterns (page 7)

1 a 3   4   5   6   7   8   9
   b −3   −1   1   3   5   7   9
   c −5   −4   −3   −2   −1   0   1
   d 3   6   9   12   15   18   21
   e 6   8   10   12   14   16   18
   f 3   7   11   15   19   23   27

2 a − 4   b × 4 + 4 or + 1 × 4
   c × 3 − 2   d × 2 − 5

Unit 3: Rules of divisibility (page 8)

1 a 1968   b 1968, 1720 and 2000
   c 1665   1845
   d 1720   1490   2000

2 a

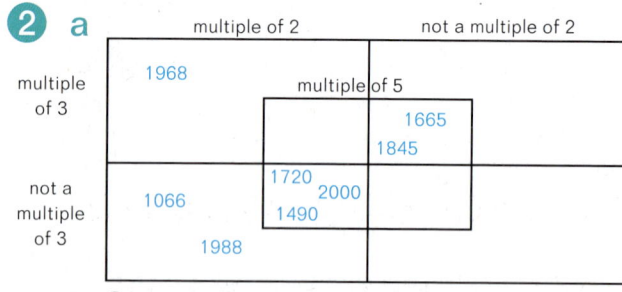

   b Check that the year is divisible by 2, 3 and 5, e.g. 1980.

Unit 4: Fractions (page 9)

1 a 8   14   20   26
   b 6   15   1   25
   c 6   3   14   24
   d 2   7   10   20
   e 10   18   40   30   66

   f 32   20   52   88   120
   g 21   60   24   72   33
   h 36   150   27   60   45

2 a $\frac{1}{4}$ of £20   b $\frac{3}{10}$ of £7
   c $\frac{3}{5}$ of £8   d $\frac{3}{4}$ of £1.60
   e $\frac{1}{5}$ of £7.20   f $\frac{7}{10}$ of £12

Unit 5: Percentages (page 10)

1 a £12.60   £32.40   £61.20   £7.38
   b £12.60   £28.20   £6.30   £3.72
   c £6   £27   £43.50   £3.60

2 Offer 1, because the discount would be £107.10.

Unit 6: Equations (page 11)

1 a 8   b 8   c 7   d 5
   e 3   f 5   g 2   h 4

2 a 9   b 15   c 9   d 3
   e 11   f 4   g 5   h 2
   i 3   j 5

3 a 22   b 14   c 10
   d 16   e 2   f 22
   g 6   h 11

Unit 7: Addition of decimals (page 12)

1 a 33.04   b 46.73   c 42.23
   d 79.56   e 62.73   f 164.61
   g 165.73   h 143.33   i 293.56
   j 91.15

2 a £44.17   b £90.66   c £143.55
   d £75.79

Unit 8: Subtraction of decimals (page 13)

1 a 19.28   b 58.36   c 32.88
   d 8.12   e 27.53   f 12.25
   g 88.48   h 47.97   i 33.76
   j 55.21

2 a £1.58   b £23.11   c £82.21
   d £9.43   e shirt and jumper

Unit 9: Multiplying decimals (page 14)

1. $0.17 \times 0.4 \rightarrow 0.068$
   0.08×7 and $0.8 \times 0.7 \rightarrow 0.56$
   8×0.7 and $0.8 \times 7 \rightarrow 5.6$
   1.7×4 and $17 \times 0.4 \rightarrow 6.8$
   $80 \times 0.7 \rightarrow 56$
   0.17×4 and $1.7 \times 0.4 \rightarrow 0.68$

2. a $\times 3 = 95.1$ b $\times 5 = 92.5$
   c $\times 9 = 105.3$ d $\times 8 = 103.2$
   e $\times 2 = 98.2$ f $\times 6 = 94.8$
   g $\times 4 = 98.8$ h $\times 7 = 100.8$

Unit 10: Multiplication: grid method (page 15)

1. a 7872   b 8694   c 25 821
   d 24 912

2. a $943 \times 76 = 71\ 668$
   b $369 \times 47 = 17\ 343$

Unit 11: Long division (page 16)

1. a 39   b 64   c 46
   d 34   e 68   f 57
   g 46   h 68

2. a 28 cm   b 18 cm   c 26 cm
   d 23 cm   e 47 cm   f 17 cm
   g 20 cm   h 36 cm

Unit 12: Lines and polygons (page 17)

Shape	Sketch	Parallel sides	All sides equal	Three or more diagonals	Right angles
Rectangle		✓	✗	✗	✓
Equilateral triangle		✗	✓	✗	✗
Rhombus		✓	✓	✗	✗
Parallelogram		✓	✗	✗	✗
Regular hexagon		✓	✓	✓	✗
Trapezium		✓	✗	✗	✗
Regular pentagon		✗	✓	✓	✗

Unit 13: 3D solids (page 18)

1. 4 rectangle faces and 2 square faces ➡ cuboid
   1 square face and 4 triangle faces ➡ square-based pyramid
   4 triangle faces ➡ tetrahedron
   6 square faces ➡ cube
   2 pentagon faces and 5 rectangle faces ➡ pentagonal prism
   2 triangle faces and 3 rectangle faces ➡ triangular prism

2.

Shape	Number of faces	Number of edges	Number of vertices
Cube	6	12	8
Cuboid	6	12	8
Tetrahedron	4	6	4
Square-based pyramid	5	8	5
Pentagonal prism	7	15	10
Triangular prism	5	9	6

faces + vertices – edges = 2

Unit 14: Symmetry (page 19)

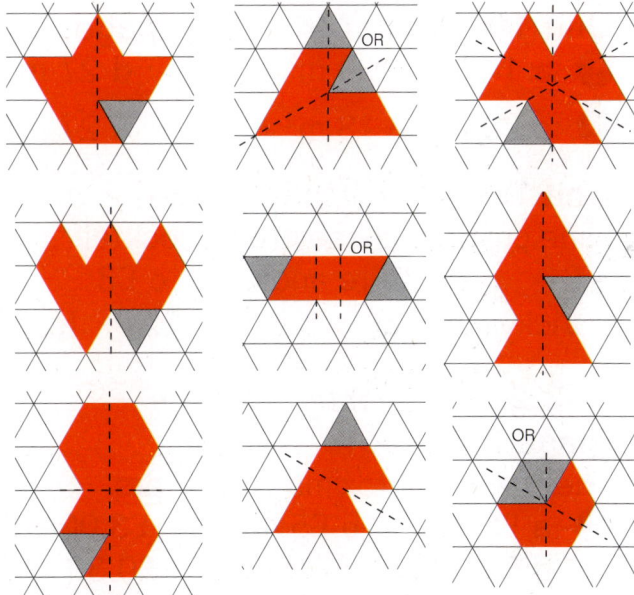

Check the colouring is symmetrical.

Unit 15: Coordinates (page 20)

1. rectangle

2. A→(–2, 3)   B→(–4, –1)
   C→(0, –3)
   D (2, 1) Check your child has plotted this correctly.

3 a A→(−3, 3) b B→(2, 3)
Check that your child has plotted the coordinates correctly and has drawn a parallelogram.

Unit 16: Measures (page 21)
1 Answers are approximate.
a 18 litres b 32 km c 4/4.05 kg
d 25 cm e 1650 ml f 2.25 kg

2

Litres	1	2.8	6	4.6	2	2.3
Pints	1.75	5	10.5	8	3.5	4

Unit 17: Timetables (page 22)
a 50 mins b 1 hour c German
d English
e 200 mins/3 hours 20 mins
f 1 hour 40 mins
g 50 mins h 100 mins

Unit 18: Area of triangles (page 23)
1 a 14 m² b 20 m² c 8 m² d 27 m²

2 a 28 m² b 18 m² c 45 m² d 27 m²

Unit 19: Pie charts (page 24)
Nine children chose prawn cocktail.
a £1 b Claire and Jack c £3
d Vicky e 50p f $\frac{1}{3}$ g £2 h $\frac{1}{4}$

Unit 20: Conversion graphs (page 25)
These are approximate answers.
1 a £2.40 b £5.40 c £3.00
d £3.60 e £1.50 f £0.30
g £4.50 h £5.70

2 a €2.00 b €8.00 c €7.00
d €10.00 e €1.50 f €3.50
g €8.40 h €6.40

3 Check that the graph is accurate.

Test 1 (pages 26 and 27)
1 a 8 8.4 b 43 42.6

2 13 17 21 Rule is × 4 − 3

3 a 1.8 metres b 100 grams
c 9 litres

4 a 360 b $\frac{1}{3}$

5 a 15 b 6

6 £2.70

7
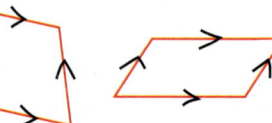 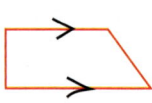 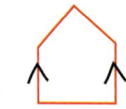

8 3.20 p.m.

9 a 26 635 b 949

10 2.63 m

Test 2 (pages 28 and 29)
1 1845

2 54 m²

3 19 737

4 a 34 b 74

5 A tetrahedron has 4 faces, 6 edges and 4 vertices.

6 a 10.8 b 0.48 c 1.92

7 £39.20

8
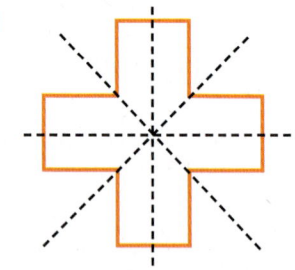

9 a $6.30 b £7.00
These are approximate answers.

Unit 1: Mnemonics

Remember

A **mnemonic** is a way of helping you to remember the spelling of difficult words.

A **miser** is always **miserable**.

Have a go

1. Fill in the missing small word to make each longer word. Read the words you make.

a te**ache**r (ache)	b be____ve (lie)	c restaur____ (ant)
_teacher_____	_____	_____
d tempe___ure (rat)	e ju____ (ice)	f choco_____ (late)
_____	_____	_____
g ve____able (get)	h im_____ant (port)	i immedi____ (ate)
_____	_____	_____
j _____ary (secret)	k _____iness (bus)	l gr____ (eat)
_____	_____	_____

2. Pick the word from the box that these sentences help you remember.

grammar	There are three **e**'s buried here. ⟶	_cemetery_
breadth	This word has **bread** in it.	_____
present	Don't **spit** on the **table**.	_____
ambitious	Without **g** this word can be spelt backwards.	_____
cemetery	If you **know** it gives you the **edge**.	_____
bicycle	Something I **sent**.	_____
hospitable	There's an **elf** in it.	_____
bargain	I **am** not a **bit** like this.	_____
twelfth	You **gain** something with one of these!	_____
knowledge	Don't ride it in **icy** weather!	_____

Unit 2: Conditional verbs

Remember

A **conditional verb** tells you the action **might** happen (or might have happened) because it **depends** on **someone** or **something else**. Some auxiliary verbs which tell you if a verb is conditional are: **should**, **would**, **could**, **might**.

I **would go** to the party if I had some nice clothes.

Have a go

1 Join up the beginnings and endings of these sentences with conditional verbs.

a If the weather stays fine	if I promise to repay you?
b I might win the Lottery	he had done his homework.
c Could I borrow some money	if I hadn't fallen down.
d She would have passed her test	we might be able to go out.
e He could not go out until	you should have a rest.
f If your friends come	if I buy a ticket.
g I might have reached the top	they would be very welcome.
h If you are tired	if she had practised more.

2 Say if the conditional verbs in these sentences indicate the past (P) or future (F) tense.

a It would cost too much to buy some new trainers. (__)

b If I go to London I might see the Queen. (__)

c I could have succeeded, with a bit of luck. (__)

d If it rains, I should not be able to go out. (__)

e If I go any faster, I might crash. (__)

f If I had looked harder, I might have found my watch. (__)

g If you come early, no-one would mind. (__)

h If I had not overslept, I would have been on time for school. (__)

Remember

Many words **end** in the same way.
Learn the spelling of some **common word endings**.
These three common word endings often **sound the same**.

diction**ary**

nurs**ery**

conservat**ory**

Have a go

1. Make some words.

ary

can**ary**   diction___   libr__   necess___   secret___
<u>canary</u>   _____   _____   _____   _____

ery

nurs___   cook___   myst___   groc___   brav___
_____   _____   _____   _____   _____

ory

laborat___   hist___   gl___   st___   vict___
_____   _____   _____   _____   _____

2. Circle the **ary**, **ery** and **ory** words in the puzzle.
   Write the meaning of the words. Use a dictionary if necessary.

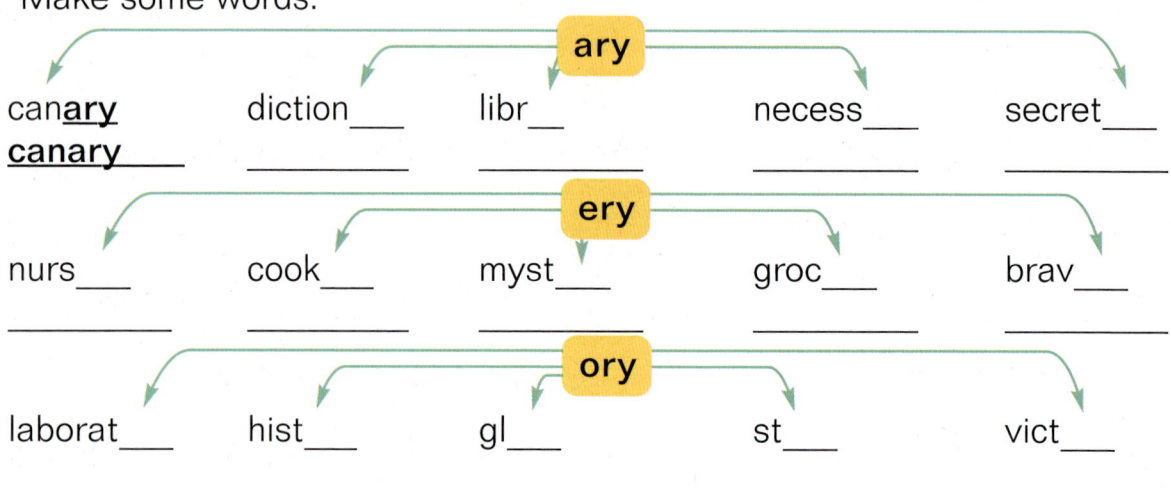

x	y	b	o	u	n	d	a	r	y	z	a
j	e	w	e	l	l	e	r	y	b	c	d
e	f	g	m	e	m	o	r	y	h	i	j
k	o	r	d	i	n	a	r	y	l	m	n
o	p	c	e	m	e	t	e	r	y	q	r
r	o	b	b	e	r	y	t	u	v	w	x
y	z	a	b	m	i	l	i	t	a	r	y

<u>a line marking the edge of some land</u>

_____

_____

_____

_____

_____

Unit 4: Abstract nouns

Remember

Abstract nouns are nouns which represent **thoughts**, **ideas** and **feelings**. You cannot touch, taste, see, hear or smell these things.

The man possessed enormous **strength**.

Have a go

1 Underline the abstract nouns in this list.

bread	honesty	car	pencil	loneliness	wonder
floor	amazement	beauty	mouse	kindness	tree

2 Write the adjective from which each of these abstract nouns comes.

a sickness **sick**   b ugliness _____   c height _____   d width _____

e heat _____   f darkness _____   g foolishness _____   h clarity _____

3 Choose the best abstract noun to complete each sentence.

tenderness   speed   danger   misery   amazement   belief   courage   power

a The knight showed considerable _____ when he fought the dragon.

b The car zoomed past at a great _____.

c There was a look of _____ in the girl's eyes.

d Emma stared at the monster in _____.

e The thief caused _____ to many people.

f The _____ of the waterfall was amazing.

g There is _____ when you cross the road.

h The astronaut had a _____ that one day he would land on Mars.

Remember

In the sentence below, the **phrase** 'with the broken window' tells us more about the noun **car**. It does the job of an **adjective** and is called an **adjectival phrase**.

The car **with the broken window** was abandoned.

Have a go

1 Choose the best adjectival phrase from the box to complete each sentence.

neat and tidy	black and curly	dark and damp
fast and sporty	rough and choppy	tall and leafy

a The girl's hair was _____.

b The tree was _____.

c My writing is _____.

d The car was _____.

e The cave was _____.

f The sea was _____.

2 Make up some sentences and use the following adjectival phrases in them.

with the blond hair
tired but happy
slim and beautiful
in the old car
long and tangled
out of breath
with the torn coat
splattered with mud

_____

_____

_____

_____

_____

_____

_____

_____

Unit 6: Spelling rules

Some **spelling rules** are helpful to remember. A good rule to learn is:

> When a word **ends** with just **one vowel** and a **single consonant**, **double** the **consonant** before **adding a suffix**.

Please begin at the begi**nn**ing!   Please control the contro**ll**er!

Have a go

1. Add **er** to these words:

a begin **beginner**   b travel _____   c signal _____

2. Add **en** to these words:

a forgot _____   b forbid _____

3. Add **ed** to these words:

a omit _____   b occur _____   c regret _____
d transmit _____   e marvel _____   f travel _____

4. Add **ing** to these words:

a fulfil _____   b admit _____   c forget _____
d prefer _____   e rebel _____   f stencil _____

5. Correct the word that is wrong in each sentence.
a You are ~~forbiden~~ **forbidden** to leave.
b I ~~omited~~ _____ to tell you something important.
c I am not ~~admiting~~ _____ to anything.
d I have ~~forgoten~~ _____ my bag.
e Tom ~~prefered~~ _____ Emma to Amy.
f The girl ~~controled~~ _____ her feelings well.
g I am already ~~regreting~~ _____ my mistake.
h The slaves took part in a ~~rebelion~~ _____.

Unit 7: Adverbs

Remember

An **adverb** tells us more about a **verb**.

The swan glided **gracefully** down the river.

Have a go

1 Choose the adverb from the box which describes the verb in each sentence.

proudly   attentively   heatedly   reverently   thoroughly   gratefully

a How people often speak in arguments. ____heatedly____

b How we should accept gifts. _____

c How a parent speaks about a successful son or daughter. _____

d How we should do our work. _____

e How we should listen to instructions. _____

f How we should behave in a place of worship. _____

2 Replace each underlined phrase with one adverb.

a The child left school (<u>in a hurry</u>) **hurriedly**_____.

b I climbed the tree (<u>with ease</u>) _____.

c We always begin a new year (<u>with hope</u>) _____.

d The gardener gazed (<u>with pride</u>) _____ at his prize roses.

e The baby's head was nodding (<u>with sleep</u>) _____.

f The woman drove her car (<u>with care</u>) _____.

g The dog was lying (<u>in peace</u>) _____ in the sun.

h The vase was broken (<u>by accident</u>) _____.

Unit 8: Unstressed vowels

Remember

Sometimes **vowels** in longer words are **not stressed**, or pronounced. These vowels are often difficult to hear.

valuable

entrance

Have a go

1 Choose the correct vowel to complete the word. Use a dictionary if necessary.

a o a

comp_ny

b o a

deodor_nt

c e a

temp_rature

d e a

marv_llous

e i e

jew_ller

f u a

marri_ge

g o a

const_ble

h a e

myst_ry

i i a

sep_rate

j u e

probl_m

k u a

cathedr_l

l e a

gen_ral

2 Choose **ar**, **er** or **or** to complete each word.

a radiat_____   b vineg_____   c cam_____a   d regul_____   e diff_____ent

f coll_____   g int_____esting   h simil_____   i project_____   j mem_____y

k min_____al   l cell_____   m north_____n   n visit_____   o err_____

3 Write the words you made in question 2 in the chart.

ar words	**er** words	**or** words

Remember

A **clause** is a **group of words** which may be used as a **whole sentence**, or as **part of a sentence**. Each clause must contain a **verb**. A **complex sentence** contains **one main clause** and one or more **subordinate** (less important) **clauses**.

The lion escaped   because the cage door was left open.

This is the **main clause**. It makes sense on its own.

This is a **subordinate clause**. It does not make sense on its own.

Have a go

1   Underline the main clause and circle the subordinate clause in each complex sentence.

a   <u>These are my new trainers</u> (that I bought yesterday.)

b   The boy was naughty when the teacher left the room.

c   My nose is red because I have a bad cold.

d   The snowman melted as soon as the sun came out.

e   Children are not allowed unless they are with their parents.

f   The flowers did not grow although I watered them.

2   Match up each main clause with a sensible subordinate clause to make a complex sentence. Underline the verb in each clause.

main clauses	subordinate clauses
It often <u>rains</u> in winter	when we visited the safari park.
The policeman caught the thief	after it had been fed.
We saw many lions	so I always <u>carry</u> an umbrella.
You can't come in	which was about her favourite singer.
The baby went to sleep	who had robbed the shop.
Mrs Smith won some money	because we played badly.
Sarah bought a magazine	unless you promise to behave.
We did not win	so she spent it on a holiday.

Remember

In English there are many common expressions which consist of **pairs of words** which often **go together**.

The two children were having a **rough and tumble**.

Have a go

1 Choose the correct word to complete each common expression.

| nonsense | means | foot | span | ruin | go | nail | shoulders |

a The thief left the shop assistant tied up **hand and** _____.
b The team fought **tooth and** _____ to win the game.
c We must think of **ways and** _____ of raising some money.
d We nearly missed the train – it was **touch and** _____.
e Tom is **head and** _____ taller than Sam.
f Mrs Hill always kept her home **spick and** _____.
g Everything the liar said was **stuff and** _____.
h The old deserted castle had been allowed to fall into **rack and** _____.

2 Choose the correct word to complete each common expression.

blood	change	starts	kin	fortune
tear	furious	easy	sound	downs
call	tongs	figures	file	sevens

a kith and _____
b beck and _____
c hammer and _____
d fits and _____
e wear and _____
f safe and _____
g rank and _____
h flesh and _____
i fame and _____
j free and _____
k sixes and _____
l facts and _____
m chop and _____
n fast and _____
o ups and _____

Remember

A pronoun is a word that **takes the place of a noun**.
We use **relative pronouns** when we refer to people, animals or things.

Anna is the small girl **who** is smiling.

We use **who** when it refers to a **person**.

I stroked the cat **which** was black.

We use **which** when it refers to an **animal** or **thing**.

Have a go

1 Choose **who** or **which** to join these pairs of clauses.

a I waved to the boy _____ was my friend.

b I could not see out of the window _____ was dirty.

c Vicky is a friend _____ is always reliable.

d I picked up my bag _____ was full of books.

e I hung up the picture _____ had fallen down.

f The man shouted at the boy _____ broke his window.

2 Use **who** or **which** to join these pairs of sentences. Write the sentences you make.

a I like my aunt. She gives me presents.
   I like my aunt who gives me presents.

b Amy looked at the sky. It was full of black clouds.
   _____

c I played with my friends. They called for me.
   _____

d Sam was smaller than his brother. His brother was older.
   _____

e My mum cleaned my bedroom. It was very untidy.
   _____

f I opened the door. It creaked loudly.
   _____

g The man picked up the coin. The coin was on the ground.
   _____

Remember

A **root** word is a word to which a **prefix** and/or a **suffix** may be **added** to make a different word.

disagree (root word – **agree**)

pronunciation (root word – **pronounce**)

Sometimes the root word is **easy** to see.

Sometimes the root word is **harder** to see.

1 Use four different colours. Colour the words which have the same roots the same colour.

grew	behaved	come	signature	given
becomes	design	misbehave	growing	
signs	growth	grow	misgiving	giver
behave	behaving	assign	behaviour	
signed	give	incoming	grows	outcome

2 Write the noun from which each adjective is made.

a disastrous   **disaster**   b cowardly   _____

c affectionate _____   d wintry   _____

e muscular   _____   f mischievous   _____

3 Write the verb from which each noun comes.

a discovery   _____   b application   _____

c entrance   _____   d permission   _____

e service   _____   f pressure   _____

Remember

We use **informal** language when we speak to each other.

Official language is often very **formal**. You find formal language on **forms**, on **notices**, in **rules** and so on.

Have a go

1 Write what each formal word means in simpler, informal language.

formal words	meaning in informal language
consume	**eat**
beverages	
forename	
reside	
dwelling	
remuneration	
forbidden	
prosecute	

2 Match up these formal and informal sentences.

formal sentences	informal sentences
State your forename in block letters.	You can't come in.
Entrance forbidden.	Slow down.
I have made an error.	Write your first name in capitals.
Access permitted.	You can pay by cheque if you want.
No trespassing on this land.	You can come in.
Restrict your speed.	Get out!
Payment by cheque permitted.	I've made a mistake.
Kindly leave the premises.	You're not allowed on this land.

Remember

Standard English is thought of as the 'correct' form of written English used in schools, business and government.

Non-standard English is often used in everyday speech.

Who's got me ball?

Who has got my ball?

This is in **non-standard** English.

This is in **standard** English.

Have a go

1 Match each pair of sentences.

non-standard English	standard English
I saw the man what done it.	I can run faster than you.
I could of eaten it easy.	Do you want a sweet?
I can run more faster than you.	I don't know anything about it.
These ain't my boots.	I saw the man who did it.
We seen him do it.	These are not my boots.
Do you wanna sweet?	All of us were hungry.
All of us was hungry.	I could easily have eaten it.
I don't know nothing about it.	We saw him do it.

2 Rewrite these non-standard English sentences in standard English.

a He should of took more care.

_____

b My teacher learned me how to swim.

My teacher taught me how to swim

c We was lucky not to get caught.

We were lucky not to get caught

d Give me one of them apples.

Give me one of those apples please

e When they come home they was muddy.

When they came home the were muddy

f Who's got me book?

Who's got my book?

g It ain't fair!

It is not fair

h I fell off of me bike.

I fell of my bike

Remember

Connectives are words or phrases that can **join** together **ideas** or **sentences**. A connective may be a **single** word or **more than** one word.

I went outside **when** it snowed.

| Connectives may come in the **middle** of a sentence. |

Firstly, plug it in. **Then** switch it on.

| Sometimes connectives come at the **beginning** of a sentence. |

Have a go

1 Circle the connectives in the middle of these sentences and underline the two clauses they join.

a I waited (while) my friend finished his tea.

b You cannot go out unless you tidy your room.

c I liked the film even though the acting was terrible.

d An apple cost 10 pence yesterday whereas today it is 15 pence.

e I can do it as often as I like.

f You can't go out because you have been misbehaving.

g I studied hard in order to pass the exam.

2 Choose the best connective to begin each sentence.

| following while firstly finally then secondly next after |

F_____, fill up a kettle with water. S_____, boil the water. W_____ it is boiling, get a cup. T_____ pour in some milk. N_____ put a tea bag in the cup.

A_____ this, pour some boiling water into the cup.

F_____ this, stir the tea and take out the tea bag.

F_____, sit down and enjoy a nice cup of tea.

Remember

New words enter our language all the time.
Eponyms are words that have originated from **people's names**.

A **guillotine** is named after Dr Joseph **Guillotin**,
who invented it during the French Revolution.

Have a go

Use a dictionary. Look up the meaning of each word.

eponym	meaning	named after
biro		a Hungarian inventor
Braille		a French teacher
cardigan		an English earl
hooligan		an English family
leotard		a French acrobat
mackintosh		a Scottish inventor
Morse code		an American inventor
pasteurise		a French chemist
wellington	a sort of boot	an English duke
dunce		an English scholar
mesmerise		an Austrian doctor
saxophone		a Belgian musician
volt		an Italian scientist

Unit 17: Prepositions

Remember

A **preposition** shows the relationship between **nouns** or **pronouns** in a sentence.

Emma apologised **to** her sister.

Have a go

1 Rewrite each of these sets of prepositions in alphabetical order:

a

behind	above	among	below	against	beside
_____	_____	_____	_____	_____	_____

b

for	down	from	off	during	into
_____	_____	_____	_____	_____	_____

c

over	through	opposite	towards	on	within
_____	_____	_____	_____	_____	_____

2 Complete each phrase with a suitable preposition:

a according _____   **b** disagree _____   **c** shrink _____   **d** guilty _____

e interfere _____   **f** aim _____   **g** ashamed _____   **h** inspired _____

i comment _____   **j** similar _____   **k** protest _____   **l** rely _____

3 Make up suitable sentences and use these phrases in them:

filled with _____

good for _____

suffer from _____

conscious of _____

divide among _____

disgusted at _____

Unit 18: Fun with words

Remember

We can learn a lot by playing **word games**. They can help with **spelling** and help improve our **vocabulary**.

radar

crate

cater

Palindromes are words that may be spelt the same **backwards** or **forwards**.

An **anagram** is a word whose letters can be rearranged to spell **another word**.

Have a go

1 Tick which of these words are palindromes.

a deed ☐	b boy ☐	c madam ☐	d girl ☐	e civic ☐
f ewe ☐	g evil ☐	h solos ☐	i sister ☐	j rotor ☐
k sock ☐	l peep ☐	m hat ☐	n toot ☐	o ruler ☐
p wow ☐	q nun ☐	r radar ☐	s pen ☐	t Anna ☐

2 Some sentences can even be palindromes! Write this sentence backwards and check!

Niagara, O roar again!

_____

3 Work out these anagrams.

a astute **statue**   b bleat _____   c bristle _____

d rubies _____   e caned _____   f scalp _____

g enlist _____   h trifle _____   i least _____

j horse _____   k smile _____   l priest _____

Unit 19: Apostrophes

Remember

We use an **apostrophe** to **show ownership**. Here are three simple rules to follow:

the boy's pen
(the pen belonging
to the boy)

the girls' shoes
(the shoes belonging
to the girls)

the children's bikes
(the bikes belonging
to the children)

> We just add **'s** to the end of all **singular** nouns.

> Many **plural nouns** end in **s**. To show ownership, we put **the apostrophe after the s.**

> When a plural noun does **not** end with **s**, we show ownership **by adding 's.**

Have a go

1 Write the shorter form of each phrase.

a the magazine belonging to Emma   Emma's magazine

b the crown belonging to the Queen   _____

c the cake belonging to Tom   _____

d the hat belonging to the woman   _____

e the tractor belonging to the farmer   _____

f the chair belonging to Mr Sharp   _____

g the beak belonging to the bird   _____

h the trunk belonging to the elephant   _____

2 Complete this chart.

longer form	shorter form with apostrophe
the ship belonging to the pirates	
the camp belonging to the soldiers	
the boots belonging to the footballers	
the toys belonging to the boys	
	the sheep's wool
	the deer's forest
	the children's swing
	the geese's eggs

Remember

Dictionaries help us **check** difficult **spellings**.

anteek ☒   anteak ☒   anteke ☒   antique ☑

Have a go

There is something wrong with each of these.
Look the words up in a dictionary. Write each word correctly.

a	proffessor	_____	b	priviledge	_____
c	neccessary	_____	d	jepordy	_____
e	parralel	_____	f	ocassion	_____
g	dissappear	_____	h	reconise	_____
i	reccomend	_____	j	fasinate	_____
k	sattelite	_____	l	exsiting	_____
m	marvelous	_____	n	restauraunt	_____
o	posession	_____	p	carrage	_____
q	comunicate	_____	r	conservatry	_____
s	suceed	_____	t	parlament	_____

Test 1

Check how much you have learned.

Answer the questions.
Mark your answers. Fill in your score.

1 Underline a small word 'hiding' inside each longer word.

believe   business

out of 2

2 Say if the conditional verbs in these sentences indicate the past (P) or future (F) tense.

a   I could have reached the top if I had tried harder. (___)

b   It would be lovely if it is hot tomorrow. (___)

out of 2

3 Choose the correct ending for each word.

a

| ary | | ery |

diction_____

b

| ory | | ary |

laborat_____

out of 2

4 Underline the two abstract nouns in this list:

car   glory   bird   house   wonder

out of 2

5 Underline the adjectival phrase in each sentence.

a   The boy with the blond hair came first.

b   The sea was calm but cold.

out of 2

6 Spell these words correctly:

a forgoten ________________

b traveler ________________

7 Replace each underlined phrase with an adverb.

a The girl danced <u>in a graceful manner</u> (____________).

b The child spoke <u>in a rude way</u> (____________).

8 Write each word correctly.
There is a vowel missing in each.

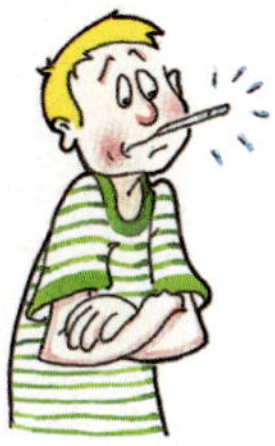

a mystry ________________

b temprature ________________

9 Underline the main clause and circle the subordinate clause in this sentence:

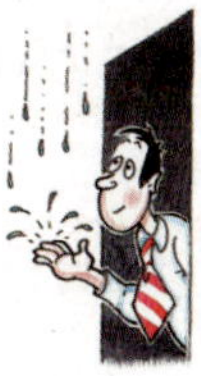

The man went indoors as soon as it rained.

10 Choose the correct word to complete each common expression.

sound **tear**

a wear and __________

b safe and __________

out of 2

out of 2

out of 2

out of 2

out of 2

Total out of 20

Check how much you have learned.

Answer the questions.
Mark your answers. Fill in your score.

SCORE

① Choose the relative pronoun **who** or **which** to complete each sentence.

a I know the woman _____ smiled at me.

b I stroked the cat _____ lived next door.

out of 2

② Write the root word of each of these longer words:

a forgiven _____

b outgoing _____

out of 2

③ Tick which informal expression matches each formal expression:

a

No trespassing

Keep out ☐

No overtaking ☐

Keep moving ☐

b Restrict your speed

Slow down ☐

out of 2

④ Rewrite each sentence in standard English.

a I could of eaten it all. _____

b Who's got me pen? _____

out of 2

⑤ Underline the connectives in these sentences.

a I practised hard in order to pass the test.

b I saved up so that I could get some new trainers.

out of 2

6 Complete each sentence correctly.

| something we eat | something we wear |

a The Earl of Cardigan gave his name to

_____.

b Lord Sandwich gave his name to

_____.

out of 2

7 Think of a sensible preposition to complete each phrase.

a to rely _____   b to interfere _____

out of 2

8 Here are some anagrams.
What other word can you make from each one?

a marble   _____

b serve   _____

out of 2

9 Write the short way of saying each of these, using apostrophes correctly.

a the book belonging to the woman

_____

b the boat belonging to the boys

_____

out of 2

10 Spell each of these words correctly. Use a dictionary if necessary.

a embarass _____

b exagerate _____

out of 2

Total out of 20

Parents' notes (English)

Unit 1: Mnemonics   There are a number of strategies your child can learn to help him or her spell better. A mnemonic is a way of helping to remember difficult words. One way is to look for smaller words 'hiding' inside longer words (e.g. there's a 'bus' in 'business'). Another way is to look for any special features in a word (e.g. there are three **e**'s in 'cemetery').

Unit 2: Conditional verbs   Verbs may be written in different forms. A conditional verb tells us that an action might happen (or might have happened) because it depends on (or is conditional upon) someone or something else. For example: I <u>would go</u> to the party if I had some nice clothes. Some auxiliary verbs which are commonly used in the conditional form are: should, would, could, might.

Unit 3: Word endings – *ary, ery, ory*   There are many common word endings. It is important for your child to recognise these when reading and to be able to use them when writing. The common word endings **ary**, **ery** and **ory** (which often sound the same) are the focus of this unit.

Unit 4: Abstract nouns   Abstract nouns are nouns that represent thoughts, ideas and feelings e.g. glory. One way of getting your child to understand these is to explain that abstract nouns are not 'concrete' and cannot be touched, tasted, seen, heard or smelt.

Unit 5: Adjectival phrases   Sometimes we may use an adjectival phrase of a few words to tell us more about the noun rather than a single adjective e.g. The car <u>with the broken window</u> was abandoned.

Unit 6: Spelling rules   Much of our spelling system is governed by logical rules. Understanding these can help your child develop sound spelling strategies. The spelling rule focused on in this unit is that when a word ends with a vowel and a single consonant, we double the consonant before adding a suffix e.g. begin + er = beginner.

Unit 7: Adverbs   Remind your child that an adverb tells us more about a verb. Adverbs of manner tell us about *how* something happened. Many of these adverbs end with the suffix **ly** e.g sadly.

Unit 8: Unstressed vowels   Some words are often misspelt because they contain vowels which are not stressed and are difficult to hear e.g. diff**e**rent, valu**a**ble. This is the focus of the activities in this unit.

Unit 9: Clauses   A clause is a group of words which may be used as a whole sentence, or as part of a sentence. A clause must contain a verb (a doing word) and have a subject (the person or thing that the verb refers to). A complex sentence contains a main clause (which always makes sense on its own) and one or more subordinate (less important) clauses which do not make sense on their own. For example: <u>The lion escaped</u> (main clause) <u>because the cage door was left open</u> (subordinate clause).

Unit 10: Common expressions   This unit introduces pairs of words which commonly go together in well-known phrases e.g. wear and tear; touch and go.

Unit 11: Pronouns   Remind your child that a pronoun is a word that takes the place of a noun. ('Pro' actually means 'in place of'.) This unit focuses on the relative pronouns 'who' (used when referring to people) and 'which' (used when referring to animals or things).

Unit 12: Prefixes and suffixes   A root word is a word to which prefixes and/or suffixes may be added at the beginning or end respectively. Sometimes the root word retains the same spelling when added to (e.g. disagreement – root word is 'agree'). Sometimes the spelling of the root word is modified in some way (e.g. 'exclamation' – root word is 'exclaim').

Unit 13: Formal and informal language   When we speak to each other conversationally, we tend to use fairly informal language. However, much 'public' language in schools, businesses, in letters, notices, signs, etc is couched in more formal terms. Your child needs to be able to distinguish between the two forms of language.

Unit 14: Standard English   Standard English is the kind of language your child is expected to use in school. In non-standard English grammatically incorrect sentences are sometimes used e.g. 'Who's got me pen?'. This unit focuses on contrasting standard and non-standard English, and correcting grammatical errors in the latter.

Unit 15: Connectives   Connectives are words or phrases that can join together ideas or sentences. A connective may be a single word or more than one word. Sometimes the connectives may come within a sentence e.g. Sarah was out of breath, <u>but nevertheless</u> (a two-word connective) she still kept running. Sometimes connectives may be used to begin sentences which are linked together e.g. <u>Firstly</u>, plug in the kettle. <u>Then</u> switch it on.

Unit 16: Eponyms   The English language is continually growing. New words are being added all the time, to describe new skills, technology, inventions etc. Eponyms are words that have originated from people's names. For example, the guillotine is named after Dr Joseph Guillotin who invented it during the French Revolution.

Unit 17: Prepositions   Prepositions often tell us about the position of one thing in relation to another. They are usually to be found in front of nouns in sentences e.g. The train went <u>through</u> the tunnel.

Unit 18: Fun with words   Encouraging your child to play and experiment with words is a good way to help him or her learn more about spelling. The activities in this unit focus on palindromes (words which may be spelt the same backwards as forwards, such as 'noon') and anagrams (words whose letters may be rearranged to make other words e.g. 'astute'/'statue').

Unit 19: Apostrophes   We use an apostrophe to show ownership. The use of apostrophes is generally poorly understood. In this unit your child is reminded of the simple rules which govern the use of the apostrophe to show ownership.

Unit 20: Using a dictionary for spelling   A dictionary is a very valuable tool. Your child needs to know how to use one. This page focuses on its function as an aid to spelling.

Answers (English)

Unit 1: Mnemonics (page 36)

1
a teacher   b believe   c restaurant
d temperature   e juice   f chocolate
g vegetable   h important   i immediate
j secretary   k business   l great

2

grammar	There are three e's buried here.	cemetery
breadth	This word has **bread** in it.	breadth
present	Don't **spit** on the **table**.	hospitable
ambitious	Without **g** this word can be spelt backwards.	grammar
cemetery	If you **know** it gives you the **edge**.	knowledge
bicycle	Something I **sent**.	present
hospitable	There's an **elf** in it.	twelfth
bargain	I **am** not a **bit** like this.	ambitious
twelfth	You **gain** something with one of these!	bargain
knowledge	Don't ride it in **icy** weather!	bicycle

Unit 2: Conditional verbs (page 37)

1
a If the weather stays fine we might be able to go out.
b I might win the Lottery if I buy a ticket.
c Could I borrow some money if I promise to repay you?
d She would have passed her test if she had practised more.
e He could not go out until he had done his homework.
f If your friends come they would be very welcome.
g I might have reached the top if I hadn't fallen down.
h If you are tired you should have a rest.

2
a F   b F   c P   d F   e F   f P   g F   h P

Unit 3: Word endings – *ary, ery, ory* (page 38)

1
can**ary**   diction**ary**   libr**ary**   necess**ary**
secret**ary**
nurs**ery**   cook**ery**   myst**ery**   groc**ery**
brav**ery**
laborat**ory**   hist**ory**   gl**ory**   st**ory**
vict**ory**

2

x y b o u n d a r y z a	a line marking the edge of some land
j e w e l l e r y b c d	decorative objects made from expensive metals and stones
e f g m e m o r y h i j	the ability to remember information
k o r d i n a r y l m n	not different, special or unexpected in any way
o p c e m e t e r y q r	area of ground where dead are buried
r o b b e r y t u v w x	the act of taking property illegally
y z a b m i l i t a r y	relating, or belonging to the armed forces

Unit 4: Abstract nouns (page 39)

1
bread   <u>honesty</u>   car   pencil   <u>loneliness</u>
<u>wonder</u>   floor   <u>amazement</u>   <u>beauty</u>
mouse   <u>kindness</u>   tree

2
a sick   b ugly   c high   d wide   e hot
f dark   g foolish   h clear

3
a courage   b speed   c tenderness
d amazement   e misery   f power
g danger   h belief

Unit 5: Adjectival phrases (page 40)

1
a black and curly   b tall and leafy
c neat and tidy   d fast and sporty
e dark and damp   f rough and choppy

2 Personal answers.

Unit 6: Spelling rules (page 41)

1
a beginner   b traveller   c signaller

2
a forgotten   b forbidden

3
a omitted   b occurred   c regretted
d transmitted   e marvelled   f travelled

4
a fulfilling   b admitting   c forgetting
d preferring   e rebelling   f stencilling

5
a forbidden   b omitted   c admitting
d forgotten   e preferred   f controlled
g regretting   h rebellion

Unit 7: Adverbs (page 42)

1
a heatedly   b gratefully   c proudly
d thoroughly   e attentively   f reverently

2
a hurriedly   b easily   c hopefully
d proudly   e sleepily   f carefully
g peacefully   h accidentally

Unit 8: Unstressed vowels (page 43)

1
a company   b deodorant   c temperature
d marvellous   e jeweller   f marriage
g constable   h mystery   i separate
j problem   k cathedral   l general

2
a radiat**or**   b vineg**ar**   c camer**a**
d regul**ar**   e diff**er**ent   f coll**ar**
g int**er**esting   h simil**ar**   i project**or**
j mem**or**y   k min**er**al   l cell**ar**
m north**er**n   n visit**or**   o err**or**

3

ar words	er words	or words
vinegar	camera	radiator
regular	different	projector
collar	interesting	memory
similar	mineral	visitor
cellar	northern	error

Unit 9: Clauses (page 44)

1
a These are my new trainers
   that I bought yesterday.
b The boy was naughty
   when the teacher left the room.
c My nose is red
   because I have a bad cold.
d The snowman melted
   as soon as the sun came out.
e Children are not allowed
   unless they are with their parents.
f The flowers did not grow
   although I watered them.

2

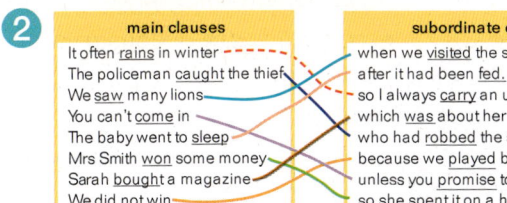

main clauses	subordinate clauses
It often rains in winter	when we visited the safari park.
The policeman caught the thief	after it had been fed.
We saw many lions	so I always carry an umbrella.
You can't come in	which was about her favourite singer.
The baby went to sleep	who had robbed the shop.
Mrs Smith won some money	because we played badly.
Sarah bought a magazine	unless you promise to behave.
We did not win	so she spent it on a holiday.

Unit 10: Common expressions (page 45)

1
a foot   b nail   c means   d go
e shoulders   f span   g nonsense   h ruin

2
a kin   b call   c tongs   d starts
e tear   f sound   g file   h blood
i fortune   j easy   k sevens   l figures
m change   n furious   o downs

Unit 11: Pronouns (page 46)

1
a who   b which   c who   d which
e which   f who

2
a I like my aunt who gives me presents.
b Amy looked at the sky which was full of black clouds.
c I played with my friends who called for me.
d Sam was smaller than his brother who was older.
e My mum cleaned my bedroom which was very untidy.
f I opened the door which creaked loudly.
g The man picked up the coin which was on the ground.

Unit 12: Prefixes and suffixes (page 47)

1

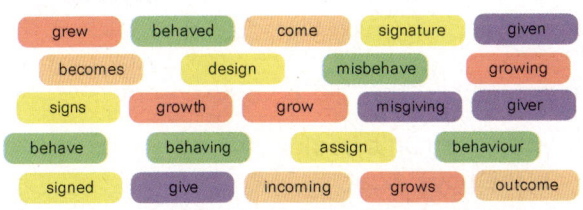

grew   behaved   come   signature   given
becomes   design   misbehave   growing
signs   growth   grow   misgiving   giver
behave   behaving   assign   behaviour
signed   give   incoming   grows   outcome

2
a disaster   b coward   c affection   d winter
e muscle   f mischief

3
a discover   b apply   c enter   d permit
e serve   f press

Unit 13: Formal and informal language (page 48)

1

formal words	meaning in informal language
consume	eat
beverages	drinks
forename	first name/Christian name
reside	live/stay
dwelling	house
remuneration	money
forbidden	not allowed
prosecute	punish someone for a crime

2

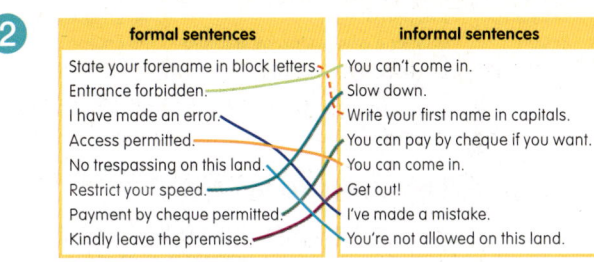

formal sentences	informal sentences
State your forename in block letters.	You can't come in.
Entrance forbidden.	Slow down.
I have made an error.	Write your first name in capitals.
Access permitted.	You can pay by cheque if you want.
No trespassing on this land.	You can come in.
Restrict your speed.	Get out!
Payment by cheque permitted.	I've made a mistake.
Kindly leave the premises.	You're not allowed on this land.

Unit 14: Standard English (page 49)

1

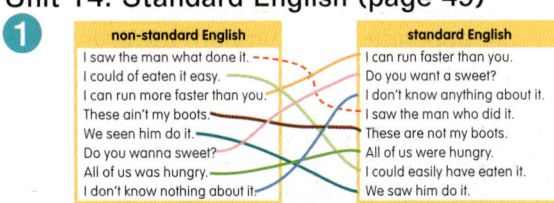

non-standard English	standard English
I saw the man what done it.	I can run faster than you.
I could of eaten it easy.	Do you want a sweet?
I can run more faster than you.	I don't know anything about it.
These ain't my boots.	I saw the man who did it.
We seen him do it.	These are not my boots.
Do you wanna sweet?	All of us were hungry.
All of us was hungry.	I could easily have eaten it.
I don't know nothing about it.	We saw him do it.

2
a He should have taken more care.
b My teacher taught me how to swim.
c We were lucky not to get caught.
d Give me one of those apples.
e When they came home they were muddy.
f Who's got my book?
g It isn't fair!
h I fell off my bike.

Unit 15: Connectives (page 50)

1
a I waited while my friend finished his tea.
b You cannot go out unless you tidy your room.
c I liked the film even though the acting was terrible.
d An apple cost 10 pence yesterday whereas today it is 15 pence.
e I can do it as often as I like.
f You can't go out because you have been misbehaving.
g I studied hard in order to pass the exam.

② **F**irstly, fill up a kettle with water. **S**econdly, boil the water. **Wh**ile it is boiling, get a cup. **T**hen pour in some milk. **N**ext put a tea bag in the cup. **A**fter this, pour some boiling water into the cup. **F**ollowing this, stir the tea and take out the tea bag. **F**inally, sit down and enjoy a nice cup of tea.

Unit 16: Eponyms (page 51)

eponym	meaning	named after
biro	a ball-point pen	a Hungarian inventor
Braille	a writing system for the blind	a French teacher
cardigan	a knitted jacket	an English earl
hooligan	a young ruffian or thug	an English family
leotard	a tight-fitting one-piece garment	a French acrobat
mackintosh	a rainproof coat	a Scottish inventor
Morse code	an alphabet represented by dots and dashes in light or sound	an American inventor
pasteurise	to partly sterilise milk by heating	a French chemist
wellington	a rainproof boot	an English duke
dunce	someone who is slow at learning	an English scholar
mesmerise	to hypnotise	an Austrian doctor
saxophone	a musical instrument	a Belgian musician
volt	a unit of force	an Italian scientist

Unit 17: Prepositions (page 52)

① a above, against, among, behind, below, beside
b down, during, for, from, into, off
c on, opposite, over, through, towards, within

② The answers below are examples. Other answers are possible.
a to   b with   c from   d of   e with   f to
g of   h by   i on   j to   k about   l on

③ Personal answers.

Unit 18: Fun with words (page 53)

① a deed ✓   b boy   c madam ✓   d girl
e civic ✓   f ewe ✓   g evil   h solos ✓
i sister   j rotor ✓   k sock   l peep ✓
m hat   n toot ✓   o ruler   p wow ✓
q nun ✓   r radar ✓   s pen   t Anna ✓

③ a statue   b table   c blister
d busier or bruise   e dance
f claps or clasp   g silent or listen
h filter   i steal or stale
j shore   k slime, limes or miles
l stripe

Unit 19: Apostrophes (page 54)

① a Emma's magazine   b the Queen's crown
c Tom's cake   d the woman's hat
e the farmer's tractor   f Mr Sharp's chair
g the bird's beak   h the elephant's trunk

②

longer form	shorter form with apostrophe
the ship belonging to the pirates	the pirates' ship
the camp belonging to the soldiers	the soldiers' camp
the boots belonging to the footballers	the footballers' boots
the toys belonging to the boys	the boys' toys
the wool belonging to the sheep	the sheep's wool
the forest belonging to the deer	the deer's forest
the swing belonging to the children	the children's swing
the eggs belonging to the geese	the geese's eggs

Unit 20: Using a dictionary for spelling (page 55)

a professor   b privilege   c necessary
d jeopardy   e parallel   f occasion
g disappear   h recognise   i recommend
j fascinate   k satellite   l existing or exciting
m marvellous   n restaurant   o possession
p carriage   q communicate   r conservatory
s succeed   t parliament

Test 1 (pages 56 and 57)

① a bel**ie**ve   b bus**i**ness. N.B. Other answers are possible.

② a P   b F

③ a dictionary   b laboratory

④ glory wonder

⑤ a The boy with the blond hair came first.
b The sea was calm but cold.

⑥ a forgotten   b traveller

⑦ a gracefully   b rudely

⑧ a mystery   b temperature

⑨ The man went indoors as soon as it rained.

⑩ a tear   b sound

Test 2 (pages 58 and 59)

① a who   b which

② a give   b go

③ a Keep out. ✓   b Slow down. ✓

④ a I could have eaten it all.
b Who's got my pen?

⑤ a I practised hard in order to pass the test.
b I saved up so that I could get some new trainers.

⑥ a something we wear
b something we eat

⑦ a on   b with

⑧ a ramble   b verse

⑨ a the woman's book
b the boys' boat

⑩ a embarrass   b exaggerate